# Cultural Intentions
# An Evidenced-based
# Framework for
# Applications of
# Cultural
# Responsiveness
# in Education

## Courtney Plotts, Ph.D.

# Copyright© 2020

# TABLE OF CONTENTS

# TABLE OF FIGURES

## Acknowledgement Page

To all the culturally responsive practitioners working each day to better the lives of students, peers, family, and friends. Especially, Lydia C. Your experiences are always on my mind.

# Chapter 1

## Culturally Responsive Teaching and Practice Challenges

Are you curious about culturally responsiveness? What is culturally responsive teaching and course design?  Responses to these questions may range from "I think I am doing ok so far" to "What is cultural responsiveness?"  Regardless of your response to this question, you can implement cultural responsiveness in your current practice. Viewing cultural responsiveness as a professional practice goes a long way in helping better support faculty, students, and staff. This means that cultural responsiveness, evidenced-based practices and systems are considered and applied throughout the current practice of teaching and course design.

Over the last twenty years, higher education institutions in the United States and Canada have significantly increased efforts to meet the needs of diverse learners attending post-secondary institutions. Students have benefited from Diversity, Equity, and Inclusion (DEI) initiatives. Although such programs are in place in many higher education institutions in the United States and Canada, systematically-marginalized individuals are, in some cases, not making the expected learning gains or are not able to function effectively in the workplace. Cultural differences in regard to educational practice require further exploration.

## What is culture?

Culture is a significant part of the human experience (Yin, 2010). Researchers suggest all research should include a cultural lens approach because it highlights the uniqueness of reported data and experiences (Hardin et al., 2014).

Various definitions of culture exist. According to Choudhury (n.d.), the following are various definitions of culture. These definitions are used in conjunction with one another and individually. The following definitions are presented because each definition adds a multi-dimensional view of culture and how it can relate to the learning environment.

**Definitions of culture** (Choudhury, n.d.):
- Culture refers to the cumulative deposit of knowledge, experience, beliefs, values, attitudes, meanings, hierarchies, religion, notions of time, roles, spatial relations, concepts of the universe, and material objects and possessions acquired by a group of people in the course of generations through individual and group striving.
- Culture is the systems of knowledge shared by a relatively large group of people.
- Culture is communication; communication is culture.

- Culture in its broadest sense is cultivated behavior; that is the totality of a person's learned, accumulated experience, which is socially transmitted, or more briefly, behavior through social learning.
- A culture is a way of life of a group of people – the behaviors, beliefs, values, and symbols that they accept, generally without thinking about them. They are passed along by communication and imitation from one generation to the next.
- Culture is symbolic communication. Cultural communication symbols include a group's skills, knowledge, attitudes, values, and motives. The meanings of the symbols are learned and deliberately perpetuated in a society through its institutions.
- Culture consists of patterns, explicit and implicit, of and for behavior acquired and transmitted by symbols, constituting the distinctive achievement of human groups, including their embodiments in artifacts; the essential core of culture consists of traditional ideas and especially their attached values; culture systems may, on the one hand, be considered as products of action, on the other hand, as conditioning influences upon further action.
- Culture is the sum of the total of the learned behavior or responses of a group of people that are generally considered the tradition of that people and are transmitted from generation to generation.

- Culture is a collective programming of the mind that distinguishes the members of one group or category of people from another.

## What is cultural responsiveness?

The New York Department of Education (2017) defines cultural responsiveness as "having an awareness of one's own cultural identity and views about difference, and the ability to learn and build on the varying cultural and community norms of students and their families." Vague definitions like this one contribute to the complexity of cultural responsiveness. This book aims to take general and vague definitions like this one and others and create a better understanding of the term cultural responsiveness.

## A robust definition

Cultural responsiveness is the ability to integrate strategies, interventions, or responses within the learning environment to improve academic outcomes for individuals whose cultural framework differs from the culture within the learning environment. Cultural responsiveness and its relationship with educational practices are emerging at best. However, there are some recognizable characteristics of cultural responsiveness besides what is mentioned in the previous definitions.

## Cultural responsiveness:

- Increases well-being
- Decreases isolation and depression
- Helps manage and reduce anxiety
- Improves socialization in academic spaces
- Acts a motivating and engagement tool
- Measurable

Additionally, cultural responsiveness is a method, and more importantly, a "prescriptive model of educational practice" that decreases the adverse effects of acculturative stress. Acculturative stress is defined as "the abrupt or enforced entry into a different and unknown cultural environment" (Brailas et al., 2015, p. 62), thus creating a psychological struggle to find social and personal balance within a novel group culture. Researchers significantly explored acculturative stress among various ethnic groups (Brailis et al., 2015; Capielo et al., 2015; Castillo et al., 2015; Hackett, 2014; Ojeda et al., 2014). High levels of acculturative stress contribute to negative patterns of coping and maladjusted behavior patterns (Glass & Westmont, 2014). Symptomology includes mild and clinical depression (Glass & Westmont, 2014). The symptoms of acculturative stress negatively impact how individuals navigate an environment.

## Why is cultural responsiveness needed?

The question of "why is cultural responsiveness needed?" is a question asked most often from resistant attendees of my trainings. It seems no one has been able to articulate what cultural responsiveness is and why so important. Vague definitions and practices leave individuals feeling like cultural responsiveness is an afterthought or optional. When in truth, it is a clinically significant aspect of successful learning experiences.

Cultural responsiveness is fundamental to instruction and course design at all levels. In some cases, common models of cultural responsiveness cause resistance to cultural responsiveness and contribute overwhelming thoughts regarding how to implement cultural responsiveness, rather than supporting more positive and applicable concepts. Current models leave many with a sense of being stuck in the middle and unsure what to do next. None of which contribute to better educational practice. So what is the answer? Why do we need cultural responsiveness? The answer is quite simple.

The reason cultural responsiveness is needed is because of something called style divergence. **Style divergence** is the idea that individuals conceptually organize learning environments in ways to make meaning and create psychological safety within a learning environment (Collier, 2005). Style divergence differs among instructors, peers, and the cultural expectations within the environment (Collier,

2011).  According to Berger, Heath, and Ho (2005), style divergence is not studied as widely as style convergence but suggests that individuals use divergent styles to distinguish themselves from "others."

Culturally responsive practitioners (CRPs) understand that style divergences allow for actual and/or perceived marginalization, racialization, racism, and microaggressions to flow through divergences.  When applied appropriately, cultural responsiveness reduces the impact of style divergences.  The reduction of divergence creates a more functional and meaningful learning environment. Collier (2011) provides the foundation for the way cultural responsiveness is needed in the learning environment.  The following list has been adapted from the work of Collier (2011) for the cultural purpose of understanding style divergence and cultural responsiveness.

1. **Style Divergence: Anxiety**
   a) An individual responds differently to challenging tasks or responsibilities than another.
   b) An individual responds differently to environmental and changes in the learning environment.
   c) Individuals do not find challenges motivating to a similar degree compared to their peers or instructor.
2. **Style Divergence: Categorization**

a) Individual uses different attributes to exclude or include similar items or experiences from a group.
b) Individuals do not separate items or experiences to similar levels of discrimination.
c) Individuals approach a task, activity, or assignment organization out of sequence versus in order as explained or outlined based on past experiences.

3. **Style Divergence: Field**
   a) Individuals approach task analysis from different perspectives. This often differs from instructor or peer expectations.
   b) Individuals perceive visual, kinetic, and auditory patterns that differ from one another.
   c) Individuals place meaning together in ways that differ from a personal approach or intentions based in lived experiences.

4. **Style Divergence: Locus of Control**
   a) Individuals show a different concept of acceptability and responsibility for actions compared to cultural expectations of the learning environment due to cultural differences in social and contextual norms.
   b) Individuals differentiate the circumstances by assigning responsibility or the locus of control. Perceptions of responsibility and locus of control differ by culture.
   c) Individuals differ in the degree of control associated with what happens to themselves within the learning environment.

5. **Style Divergence: Persistence**
   a) Individuals differentiate the length of time required to concentrate and focus on a task or solve a problem.
   b) Individuals use or maintain a different level or degree of self-monitoring than the academic culture expects.
   c) Individuals differentiate concepts like comfort levels or perceived importance associated with meeting deadlines and getting work on time.

6. **Style Divergence: Tolerance**
   a) Individuals demonstrate different levels of comfort with fantasy than expected within the learning environment.
   b) Individuals have different approaches to using their imagination in educational experiences and learning tasks.
   c) Individuals show a different response (level of comfort) to reality-based tasks, content, or learning than the culture expects.

**Style Divergence: Tempo**
   a) Individuals differ in level or degree of comfort with the pace of learning and teaching expected within the learning environment.
   b) Individuals are more impulsive or cautious with answers, tasks, and problem solving than the learning environment expects.
   c) Individuals need differing amounts of time to consider the correctness of a response than what the learning environment expects.

For educators unfamiliar with culturally responsive practices, such differences can create significant frustration, distrust, lack of empathy, and resistance within the learning environment. For CRPs, the divergence creates an opportunity to implement the appropriate culturally responsive practices that support learning. Culturally responsive learning environments consider concepts such as:

- **Communal competence:** The ability to create and sustain relationships and perceive and transmit empathy throughout a learning community.
- **Resourcefulness:** The ability to problem-solve and recognize creative and constructive thinking related to collective cultural norms.
- **Altruism:** One's ability to weigh the risk to oneself or others around them.
- **A sense of purpose:** The ability to build or perceive a more positive future than the present.

Cultural responsiveness is also one's ability to observe and acknowledge levels of cultural variance, and bridge the gaps of culture that contribute to adverse outcomes. Identifying divergences is a foundational aspect of culturally responsive practice.

## Working Models of Culture and Current Theory

When most individuals think of culture, they think of ethnic culture. Ethnic culture and culture associated with intersectionality (LGBTQ/Feminism, etc.) are important components of cultural responsiveness. To effectively apply cultural responsiveness, practitioners have to develop an understanding of the four other areas of culture in the learning environment that are influenced by or create or illicit cultural responses from those within the environment. There are five essential crucial cultural responsiveness areas: Academic Culture, Collaborative Culture, Cognitive Culture, Community Culture, and Ethnic and Intersectionality Culture (ACCCE).

*Figure 1 - Academic Culture, Collaborative Culture, Cognitive Culture, Community Culture, and Ethnic Culture (ACCCE)*

A pattern of cultural response occurs within each culture. These responses are from peer-to-peer, peer-to-course, and instructor-to-student. Let's take community culture as an example. Let's suppose that an individual shows a different concept of acceptability and responsibility for actions compared to cultural expectations of the learning environment related to the community culture' (style divergence: anxiety).  If cultural responsiveness is not considered, one or more of the following is likely to occur:

**Peer-to-peer:**  A student who struggles in a course does not feel comfortable asking the instructor for help.  The student is reluctant to reach out to peers for help because there are no cues for a sense of community within the course.

A faculty member or instructional designer of color continually struggles with imposter syndrome and acculturative stress because they work in a predominately white institution.  They are overwhelmed by cultural taxation and suffer in silence.  There are familiar cues for a sense of community within that environment.

**Peer-to-course:**  A student struggles to understand course material but does not feel comfortable asking the instructor for help.  The course does not affirm the value of community and interdependence. The student does not feel comfortable reaching out to peers due to the lack of community considerations. The student stops participating in the course but does not drop the course.

**Employee-to-course:** A staff member of color is completing a new employee training.  But there is no mention of cultural taxation and health and wellness that relates to racialized and cultural burdens within the employee organization. The is however, multiple mentions regarding racism, microaggression, and oppression. There is no mention of resources available to support the effects such concepts.

**Instructor-to-student:** A faculty member is frustrated and states that students are "lazy" and want students to be autonomous in their learning, but the online course does not outline the virtual pathway to build, support, and maintain a sense of community for students to discuss the difficulties within the course.

Examples like the ones above continually occur because there is no consideration or understanding of cultural responsiveness. Current culturally responsive practices are more generalized and topical responses. However, an evidenced-based and measurable model of cultural responsiveness is warranted. The idea of an evidenced-based measurable can provide a more precise application of cultural responsiveness. The important thing to remember is there is a lot more to applying cultural responsiveness than is generally presented in most learning experiences.

**What makes cultural responsiveness so complex?**

Like culture, cultural responsiveness is also a complex concept. In addition to the vagueness of current models, the lack of definitions surrounding cultural responsiveness, and a clear understanding of why cultural responsiveness is needed and its effective application is often elusive. Culture is a complex phenomenon in concept and practice. The complex nature of cultural responsiveness makes for elusive application practices.

Complexity of cultural responsiveness is often used as a barrier implementing cultural responsiveness in a learning environment. Such barriers make it difficult to "adopt culturally linked competencies and develop culturally responsive teaching and design practices" (Alankhunona et al., p.65).

Conceptually, culture is a multifaceted set of values, norms, attributes, languages, and customs with specific meanings for individuals aligned with a particular cultural group. Ideally, culture is a phenomenon we celebrate to highlight the uniqueness and value of individuals around us.

Consider the following:

- Each individual has a uniqueness that only they bring into the learning experience.
- Each individual has an identity and lived experiences only they can bring into the learning experience.
- Each individual requires different levels of cultural responsiveness to engage in a learning community actively.

Theoretically, the emphasis on culture happens implicitly and explicitly within the educational, social, and psychological experiences because cultural responsiveness and competence would be highly prioritized. However, researchers have shown that "educators who possess high cultural competence levels do not translate into confidence with cultural responsiveness" (Mareno & Hart, 2014, p.83).

In practice, a disconnect exists between cultural competency and cultural responsiveness. This disconnect adds to the complexities and often inspires further resistance to application of cultural responsiveness. This resistance is often motivated by frustration, anger, feelings of worry, doubt, guilt, and uncertainty by practitioners who further contribute to the barriers to applying cultural responsiveness in one's practice. This can lend insight, for understanding why some people are so resistant to having the conversation about cultural responsiveness and its application within educational spaces.

The complexities of cultural responsiveness additionally create barriers for students. Campbell (2015) suggested the absence of cultural responsiveness increases the potential for discrimination and acculturative stress in learning experiences. The lack of recognition for those barriers leads to Eurocentric values that translate into oppressive perspectives toward Non-European American students (Booker et al., 2015). Eurocentric culture is the dominate culture within educational practice.

The lack of consideration for cultural responsiveness contributes to high levels of cultural taxation among faculty of color. Cultural taxation is the "unique burden placed on faculty of color in carrying out their job responsibility to the service of a higher education institution" (Canton, 2012, p.10). Cultural taxation is why it is important to consider cultural responsiveness beyond the classroom and with a student focus. Cultural responsiveness should be a concept expanded throughout educational systems because it can benefit everyone regardless of title.

To illustrate the point of uniqueness and highlight outcomes associated with a vague understanding of cultural responsiveness and its relationship to cultural taxation, Pratt (2020) interviewed Mario Pile, the Assistant Director of Development at Boise State. Pile noted that the following examples could undo the burden of cultural taxation:

- "Have a person of color speak on a topic related to business, higher education, politics – anything that doesn't have to do with diversity and inclusion."
- Don't just pick one person to be the unofficial spokesperson for anything diversity-related.
- "I want to share the wealth with my brothers and sisters. I know a lot of talented young black men and women who I want to give recognition to and

see them do things equally."

- Don't label those people of color as 'resources,'
  but 'label them as humans like everyone else.'
- Address the cultural taxation: "It's like biases.
  "Let's acknowledge that it exists. It's complex."

## Cultural Responsiveness in Online Spaces

We cannot forget about online learning spaces. The complexity of cultural responsiveness also influences online and hybrid environments (Plotts, 2020; 2020; Soper & Ukot, 2016; Dzumbinzki, 2014). Although everything discussed up to this point applies in the online setting, online learning has a specific culture. Opportunities for practitioners to develop cultural responsiveness significantly limit online instructors' ability due to lack of proximity, lack of collaboration, and need for travel for face-to-face collaboration for most meaningful culturally responsive professional developments (Chin, 2013; Heightener, & Jennings, 2016).

However, in 2020, due to a worldwide pandemic, we have reimagined professional development for educators. The importance of cultural responsiveness in online spaces gained more consideration when millions took up virtual and digital communications to sustain or increase their presence in vital business and personal interactions. With that said, online education professionals face challenges because cultural responsiveness is in more nebulous virtual learning spaces than in face-to-face spaces.

Similar to face-to-face learning experiences, online practitioners facilitate, build, maintain, and sustain relationships among members of the online learning community (Soper & Ukot, 2016). Instructors are also responsible for facilitating meaningful connections between students and course content. Building a culturally inclusive atmosphere requires understanding community members and their ethnic and cultural norms (Dzubinski, 2014). Online learning environments are limited to ethnic and cultural cues (Brailis et al., 2016), but some cultural cues exist (Plotts, 2018). Carter (2015) found individuals could identify ethnicity in virtual spaces because ethnic exchanges are associated with specific levels of 'intensity,' enabling people to ethnically identify and relate to one another while also creating a solid self-identity within online spaces (Prause & Mujtaba, 2015). A culturally responsive practitioner can recognize these attributes to build and sustain healthy collaborative and social experiences with cultural considerations to facilitate meaningful learning experiences (Heightner & Jennings, 2016).

The absence of such considerations leads to adverse psychological and academic outcomes for systematically marginalized and racialized student populations. This is because there is an absence of affirmation, social acceptance, and psychological well-being within the applied theoretical frameworks currently used to further best practices in online spaces.

## Culture Presence: The Co-framework to Teaching and Design Models

The Community of Inquiry Theory (COI) is synonymous with online learning. COI also applies to face-to-face teaching, also (Warner, 2016). According to Warner (2016), in the application of COI, a face-to-face setting was associated with positive outcomes such as "deeper conversations, participation and in classwork" (p. 436). The community of inquiry theory consists of three domains of learning teaching presence, cognitive presence, and social presence.

What builds success within this framework? The literature is pretty clear. Independent learning, self-efficacy, and self-identity are frequently associated with online learning culture and distinct cultural norms. These terms align with individualistic cultural norms and the struggle of ethnically diverse learners who identify with communal cultural norms to find a place. Ethnic culture influences social and learning experiences (Aronson & Laughter, 2016; Booker et al., 2016; Campbell, 2015).

Community of Inquiry creates robust learning and social interactions (Whiteside, 2014). Community of Inquiry is associated with online learning best-practices and consists of three interconnected aspects of online learning: cognitive presence, social presence, and teaching presence (Garrison, 2000; Garrison et al., 2010). Cognitive presence is one's ability to make meaning of academic content

(Garrison et al., 2010). Social presence is the psychological and social attribute of online spaces. Teaching presence is the skill of facilitation and delivery of curriculum and content in online spaces (Garrison et al., 2010).

Although COI is a model of best practices for teaching and learning practices, the influences of ethnicity and culture on the social, psychological, and cognitive presence as well as student experiences are not represented within the model, nor do any previous studies list this absence as a limitation. Communal cultural norms differ significantly from an online learning culture, such as independence and self-focus. Cultural differences increase acculturative stress among systematically marginalized and racialized student populations (Cox-Davenport, 2014).

Best practices contribute to marginalization and isolation among underrepresented students taking classes because cultural responsiveness is absent. To help foster a better understanding of the cultural aspects of COI, a model of cultural presence is presented to increase the cultural scope of the COI framework. Cultural presence is the intentional inclusion, use, and application of ethnic and cultural norms within the teaching and learning process that supports learning, student well-being, and meaningful outcomes. "Cultural presence applies to teaching and learning, course design, and the student socialization in the online space" (Plotts, 2018, p. 2). There are five aspects of course design and teaching that construct cultural presence:

- Intentionality
- Transactional versus relational course design
- Convergent versus divergent thinking
- Collaboration and contextual learning
- Independent versus interdependent learning

*Figure 2 - Cultural Presence Model*

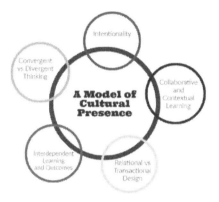

Intentionality is one's ability to understand the how and why of what is occurring in their online space. Researchers noted the faculty's specific and intentional focus is required for knowledge and skill regarding culturally responsive teaching (Soper & Ukot, 2016). To facilitate cultural presence in online spaces, faculty require specific training in areas such as effective collaboration across cultures, building and maintaining community, and fostering appropriate learning climates in virtual spaces with the use of culturally responsive models of teaching (Plotts, 2020).

Current design models of teaching are transactional and contribute to significant barriers to creating human connection. Transactional connections in online spaces are orchestrated and quantified (e.g., week one: post once, respond twice). Alternatively, faculty can focus on the relational nature of information delivery and exchanges by building a sense of community and course climate. This focus creates more meaningful connections between students and their peers, as well as students and course content.

Independent learning is often associated with online learning outcomes. But the concept of independence or individuality is Eurocentric in nature. Instead, creating a cultural presence focuses on the interdependence of learning for students in online spaces. In addition, cultural presence applies opportunities such as social modeling, building peer support, and increasing interconnectedness as cultural norms within the online course.

Academic culture is often associated with one's ability to think critically. For example, Garrison et al. (2010) originally placed more value on the cognitive presence (critical thinking) than on social and teaching presence. They noted that cognitive presence, social presence, and teaching presence were equivalent and contributed equally to learning outcomes in online spaces.

Collaborative cultures often prefer divergent (creative and imaginative) thinking and identify this manner of thinking as something valued more than convergent (critical) thinking. Applying the model of cultural presence within an online course increases the opportunity for divergent thinking within the teaching and learning process.

Collaborative and contextual learning align with best practices for social learning. The current COI and collaboration models rarely highlight the role culture plays in communal experiences. Current models omit the importance of how ethnic student groups use cultural norms to position themselves in collective social experiences. This absence of cultural norms contributes to negative experiences for underrepresented populations. Social positioning via cultural norms is essential for minoritized students working collaboratively in online spaces (Maldonado-Torres, 2014).

Cultural presence is an essential facet of effective teaching and learning. Community psychology, multicultural psychology, and learning and cognition researchers highlight the importance of effective culturally responsive education for minoritized student groups. The lack of culturally responsive teaching in online spaces contributes to acculturative stress among student populations. Using this model of cultural presence for online spaces can support faculty and instructional designers in creating robust learning experiences for students of different ethnic groups.

## Becoming a Stronger Practitioner

**A question:** How did you move from beginner to expert in your professional career?  It was probably a gradual process that took time, patience, skill-building, and understanding.  It also likely required personal motivation and an intentional effort on your part.

Gradual learning or scaffolded instruction (Wood et al., 1766) is often associated with theoretical teaching models, course design, and learning.  The theories of social learning theory (Bandura, 1971) and cognitive structuring (Piaget, 1971) are a few examples.  Each theory supports the follow ideas about learning:

- Learning happens collaboratively
- Intentional interaction is critical to the teaching and learning process
- Specific techniques are required in a specific pattern for the most effective outcomes to occur
- Targeted strategies implemented during the teaching and learning process support continual learning and understanding

Developing and applying culturally responsive techniques require intentionality on the practitioner's part (Plotts, 2021; Soper & Ukot, 2016; Dzumbinski, 2014; Hackett, 2012).  A desire to be culturally responsive comes from within (Soper & Ukot, 2016).  A person must desire to apply cultural responsiveness to their framework. If you are reading this book, you are likely a person who desire more cultural responsiveness in your professional scope. So let's keep reading.

**What happens when cultural responsiveness is disregarded, minimized, or simply not applied within the learning environment?**

The answer to this question is simple. I am sure you are familiar with *Newton's Law: For every action, there is an equal and opposite reaction.* The same is true for cultural responsiveness. For every cultural response or that lack thereof, there is a counter-response. Cultural responsiveness, or the lack thereof, solicits one or more of four psychological responses from individuals. The four responses associated with high levels of acculturative stress and low levels of cultural responsiveness are assimilation, integration, separation, and marginalization.

Each response requires unique cultural responses to address the psychological presented within the learning environment. More specifically, responses that reflect: (1) ethnic/intersectionality culture, (2) a support of communal learning, and (3) alternatively selecting separation or marginalization as responses in the learning environment.

Experts have noted positive results when including culturally responsive strategies (Booker et al, 2015; Traindis,1994; Dzumbinski, 2014). Developing culturally relevant interpersonal communication in the learning environment is critical to cultural responsiveness (Campbell, 2014). Psychological attributes associated with culturally responsive teaching increase positive outcomes among ethnically diverse learners in online settings by decreasing acculturative stress (Heightner & Jennings, 2016).

According to the IRIS Center at Vanderbilt University (2021), cultural responsiveness is an ongoing process of:

- Understanding that culture has a role in education
- Actively learning about students' cultures and communities
- Learning about the beliefs and values of various cultures, regardless of those cultures represented in the class
- Broadening their awareness and gaining insight into issues facing diverse students, families, and communities

In truth, there is much more to cultural responsiveness than outlined by most centers for learning and faculty development centers. Additional considerations will be addressed in future chapters.

## The Biggest Challenge to Cultural Responsiveness

To this point, we have discussed the culture, cultural responsiveness, and the complexities of both. At best, an unclear and shadowy application of cultural responsiveness occurs within higher learning institutions. But, one big challenge remains. The complexities of "diversity and concepts of cultural competence are not always clearly integrated into curricula and design practices" (Diaz, Clark, and Gutua, 2015, p. 22).

To solve this problem, a clear and concise framework for cultural responsiveness is needed to validate culturally responsive practices further. The absence of a framework creates questions like: How do practitioners change? How do practitioners effectively apply cultural responsiveness tied to desired outcomes? How do we effectively design, educate, introduce, and document our culturally responsive teaching and design efforts? How do we know what frequency, techniques, and design strategies work most effectively? How do we know if our cultural responsiveness is working in the environment? When does the practitioner stop one approach and start another? Practitioners apply broad and arbitrary 'cues' of cultural responsiveness in their courses and content … without knowing their impact. We will answer these questions in the following chapters.

## Putting It Together

Cultural responsiveness. It's complicated. In Latin, the word responsiveness means 'to pledge again.' One's value of culture depends on various factors associated with one's willingness and ability to increase cultural competency and cultural framework (Booker et al., 2015).

At best, cultural responsiveness is applied randomly in institutions across the United States. Generalized understanding are applied to human experiences with little consideration of the the complexities of culture and the effectiveness for students and professionals.

We start where we began. Does the term cultural responsiveness mean something different to you now? For whom is the learning environment created? Everyone? No one? Or just a few?

Applications of cultural responsiveness must be intentional, meaningful, and culturally explicit to the learning environment and the lived experiences of designers, faculty, and students. Practical applications of cultural responsiveness require intent, understanding, and practical methods to reach learning goals purposely.

# Chapter 2

## Barriers and Measurement of Cultural Responsiveness

People make assumptions when thinking about success. Particularly, when culture and success are mentioned. Culture shapes the way individuals respond to social and learning opportunities within the learning environment. As stated earlier in chapter one, individuals react differently to change and expectations. This is where people begin to reference factors like grit, determination, and self-efficacy (which are outdated). In other words, if someone can tap into their skill set of superpowers, they will be successful.

Additionally, it is offensive to suggest "grit" to people who associate with ethnic groups who survived a systematic geocide. Many indigenous communities come to mind. The fact that communities have survived in spite of a systematic genocide, should highlight levels of "grit", "determination", and "self-efficacy." Deconstructing barriers is almost impossible due to the omission of cultural responsiveness in many cases. The current practices of "success" create four common obstacles to cultural responsiveness and social and practical learning.

## Barrier 1: Assumptions

We assume individuals can succeed regardless of circumstances within our current frameworks and institutional systems. Individuals from all socio-economic classes face challenges in the professional and educational setting. Bullying, depression, anxiety, isolation, and feelings of inadequacy are prevalent as well as 'imposter syndrome' are commonly associated with juxtaposed racial and cultural differences. Such feelings do not fall solely along ethnic and racial lines. However, those feelings can originate from experiences of racism, marginalization, microaggression, and prejudice among individuals of color and those from systemically marginalized communities.

The rejection of cultural responsiveness practices significantly limits academic success (Booker et al., 2015). Moreover, systematically marginalized and racialized people may not select assimilation as a way to be successful because of the negative influences associated with the host culture (the culture individuals move into). The rejection of cultural responsiveness also contributes to a rapid increase in acculturative stress and provides a platform for unhealthy exchanges between individuals when a power dynamic is present.

## Barrier 2: Lack of Affirmation

Educators may fail to identify, recognize, and support individuals who experience acculturative stress. Strong self-concept, identity, and efficacy have been tied to affirmation within the learning environment and contributes to the decrease of acculturative stress. For instance, this is why something like representation matters.

A diverse representation of students affirms their likeness and value within the learning space. Affirmation occurs in the learning environment prior to someone providing self-affirmation. In other-words, generalized affirmation help builds self-affirmation. Self-affirmation supports improvements in executing functioning, e.g., attention, thinking, knowledge, and perception (Harris, Harris, & Miles, 2017). Little research has been conducted on affirming strategies in higher education. Representation has been significantly discussed, which is most often referred to as visual affirmation or representation of diversity, equity, and inclusion.

## Barrier 3: Limited Access to Formal Assessment and Culturally Responsive Practitioners

According to the Labor Department in the United States (2020), the counseling and psychology profession is predominately white.

*Figure 3 - United States Department of Labor, Bureau of Labor Statistics, 2020 Ethnic Breakdown*

| https://www.bls.gov/cps/cpsaat18.htm | 2020 | | | | | |
|---|---|---|---|---|---|---|
| | Total Employed | Women | White | Black or African American | Asian | Hispanic |
| Education and health services | 34,105 | 74.6 | 75.7 | 14.8 | 6.3 | 13.2 |
| Educational services | 13,369 | 69.5 | 80.7 | 10.8 | 5.4 | 12.5 |
| Elementary and secondary schools | 8,671 | 75.7 | 82.6 | 11.6 | 3.1 | 13.6 |
| Colleges, universities, and professional schools, including junior colleges | 3,772 | 55.4 | 75.7 | 10.2 | 10.4 | 10.1 |
| Business, technical, and trade schools and training | 77 | 57.8 | 84.9 | 5.8 | 7.9 | 14.1 |
| Other schools and instruction, and educational support services | 850 | 69.8 | 83.8 | 6.7 | 6.5 | 11.1 |

Additionally, counselors and psychologists are not well-versed or trained in the nuances of culture and are quick to note that anxiety is generalized rather than culturally specific. The lack of mental health providers originating from marginalized populations contributes to the continuation of acculturative stress in learning environments. "Individual experiences noticed cultural responsiveness was conspicuously absent from their therapists' knowledge base included issues such as racism and discrimination"(Mendel-son, Turner, Tandon, 2010, p. 887). To add another consideration, mental health professionals of color have been trained in a Eurocentric framework and are just more recently exploring culturally responsive counseling applications in higher education.

## Barrier 4: Diversity vs. Disability

According to Collier (2011), educators have difficulty identifying cultural differences and often confuse or conflate them for learning disabilities. Equally as problematic, learning disabilities may be generalized to cultural differences. In reality, culturally responsive teaching and design strategies provide clarity where there is confusion. Understanding cultural interventions and strategies for cross-culturally teaching have a significant outcome for systematically marginalized student groups.

As stated earlier in Chapter 1, there is a human response to every desire or lack of cultural responsiveness. Below are four responses that individuals use to respond to varying levels of acculturative stress.

## Response 1: Climb Over or Fight Through the Barrier

Even though it may be psychologically detrimental, many individuals opt to work through the barrier. Individuals can quickly identify a cultural barrier and will work through the challenge. Some individuals take working through the challenge as a point of pride that a larger system could not stop them or hold them back from their accomplishments. This perseverance does not mean the individuals do not experience negative experiences within the culture or that they did not experience a culture change. On the contrary, such individuals may have experienced more negative experiences yet still persisted in their academic or professional pursuits. One's ability to select this approach is often rooted in personality, self-efficacy, and social support.

## Response 2: Acculturative Stress

How do you deal with stress? Do you exercise? Do you chat with friends or maybe go out to dinner? Do you pet your cat? Do you struggle to think happy thoughts even when it is near impossible? Perhaps if you are an introvert, you find places inside you didn't know you had. If you are an extrovert, do you find yourself with an insatiable need to be around people, but you are not sure why. Or, perhaps you fall somewhere in between. These are your self-selected responses to cope with stress. Although it may happen consciously or unconsciously, you attempt to cope with the stress that may or may not be evident to you or those around you.

The American Psychological Association (2020) noted individuals use specific strategies to manage their contact (that causes acculturative stress) with and participation in the culture of a larger, dominant group (APA, 2020). In other words, people can self-select (consciously or subconsciously) how they will 'manage' the impact of acculturative stress in the environment.

At times, individuals select strategies to deal with acculturative stress. As a reminder from chapter one, Acculturative stress is defined as "the abrupt or enforced entry into a different and unknown cultural environment" (Brailas et al., 2015, p. 62), thus creating a psychological struggle to find social and personal balance within a novel group culture. Researchers significantly explored acculturative stress among various ethnic groups (Brailis et al., 2015; Capielo et al., 2015; Castillo et al., 2015; Hackett, 2014; Ojeda et al., 2014). High levels of acculturative stress contribute to negative patterns of coping and maladjusted behavior patterns (Glass & Westmont, 2014). Symptomology includes mild and clinical depression (Glass & Westmont, 2014).

Acculturative stress leads to high levels of attrition (Bai, 2014), non-attendance, low levels of student retention, and lower grade point averages (GPAs) were associated with acculturative stress (Jenkins et al., 2013). For educational professionals, it leads to high levels of isolation, depression, frustration, and feelings of defeat. Researchers have also associated acculturative stress with decreased self-efficacy, self-image, and self-directed learning and socialization (Altugan, 2015; Mykota, 2014).

## Response 3: Four Strategies of Responding to Acculturative Stress

According to Rudmin (2003) and other social science researchers, individuals self-select strategies to cope with assimilation, integration, separation, and marginalization. These strategies are called adaptive acculturative responses. The responses occur due to changes social changes in the learning environment. These are called adaptive cultural responses. The four responses are:

**Assimilation:** The complete adoption and absorption of a culture.

- Assimilation individuals fully adopt and understand the culture within the learning (Brailis et al., 2015).

For instance, if an individual selects the strategy of assimilation, they may be familiar with the academic culture, and their brain is open to learning because they do not feel the need to protect themselves within that culture. This is because they are comfortable and familiar with the learning process and the associated educational and social culture. However, the institution at large may contribute to feelings of marginalization.

**Integration:** When individuals maintain their cultures and accept and adapt to the host's cultures.

- Individuals who select integration somewhat accept the learning environment's culture yet retain their cultural identity.

***Separation****:* When individuals become alienated toward the host culture and separate themselves from the majority society.

- Learners mainly prefer to socialize with persons from their own culture (Brailas et al., 2015).

Individuals who select separation and integration fall between learning and lifeguarding in the cognitive process. The differing responses to acculturative stress naturally require different responses and techniques at varying intensities to decrease the multiple levels of acculturative stress. Research supports historical aspects of systemic racism and negative experiences with acculturation (Menon, & Harter, 2012).

***Marginalization (Deculturation):*** When individuals become alienated from their own and host cultures (Culhane, 2004).

- The marginalized student does not participate but does not drop the course (Brailas et al., 2015).

When individuals use marginalization to respond to acculturative stress, they have significantly more difficulty accessing effective learning experiences. Much of the cognitive bandwidth for learning is occupied not by the learning, thinking, or memory, but instead, the brain is tasked with self-preservation or 'lifeguarding.' Lifeguarding occurs when individuals perceive high levels of racism, prejudice, microaggressions, alienation, and/or isolation. Psychological and social self-protection becomes the main cognitive process. It is difficult for the brain to learn and lifeguard at the same time.

Like the term assimilation, the term marginalization (deculturation) is used more in the sociological context as a verb. For example, someone might say, "Our local community is marginalizing X group of people" for X reason. This is also an appropriate use of the term marginalization and is true in larger social contexts.

Marginalization (deculturization) is detrimental to human psychological and social experiences (Ng et al., 2013). Some individuals select marginalization as a method of managing acculturative stress. Individuals may also experience marginalization through encounters with the host culture (Benabdallah & Jolibert, 2013). Engaging with dominant host cultures includes social interactions, including discrimination, stereotyping, and racism (Benabdallah & Jolibert, 2013). Systematically marginalized and racialized individuals reported similar experiences with marginalization within higher education institutions (Carss et al., 2015; Petty, 2014).

Although individuals may select marginalization as a method of managing or responding to acculturative stress or the lack of cultural responsiveness in the environment, the same individuals may also experience marginalization through everyday encounters within the host culture (Benabdallah & Jolibert, 2013).

Engaging with dominant host cultures has often included social interactions, including discrimination, stereotyping, and racism (Benabdallah & Jolibert, 2013). Systematically marginalized and racialized learners reported similar experiences with marginalization within higher education settings (Carss et al., 2015; Petty, 2014). Experiences included macroaggression, stereotyping, and discrimination (Booker et al., 2015).

According to Hoffman (2003), more significant systemic issues take years to foster change. Hoffman (2003) suggested that the social change in the context of healthcare and education in American history often takes years and starts at the grassroots level. When systemic change occurs slowly, practitioners feel overwhelmed by the amount of work still to get done. Focusing on strategies as responses to acculturative stress created from the style divergence and a lack of cultural responsiveness in addition to, a larger social context for teaching, learning, and course design is imperative to support systemic change.

Although the social context concepts are a current reality and more than relevant, and essential to understanding within a greater social and systemic context, the definitions shared above solely focus on the individual's selection as a psychological response to coping with acculturative stress and its impact on learning outcomes. The repeated application of teaching, course design, and social learning theory void of cultural considerations of acculturative stress have caused individuals to select one of the four responses listed above as a response to the lack of cultural responsiveness in the environment.

## Response 4: Familiarity

Most humans are creatures of habits in one or more areas of their lives. In most instances, humans prefer patterns of comfort and/or consistency. Things we are comfortable with are not always healthy for us. And in most instances, do not turn out well in the end.

*\*\*TRIGGER WARNING. SKIP IF NEEDED. \*\**

*Take our most unpleasant relationship break up, for instance. We may have stayed in the relationship longer than we needed to because it was a comfortable situation most of the time. We probably needed to leave six months prior or more. The question is, why did we stay longer? Friends told us to leave. We saw the signs ourselves, but inevitably we stayed. Why? Familiarity, comfort, and ease. These concepts play a significant role in our decision-making when change is involved.*

Familiarity is why some people, at times, select marginalization as a response to acculturative stress.

Again, for clarity, this is not someone accepting marginalization from the larger system, but rather as a response to one of the biproduct the system creates (acculturative stress). Automatic responses occur partly because the response is comfortable and familiar to a person. It has worked to manage the stress in the past.

Repeated exposure to marginalizing practices and marginalizing institutions such as under-performing schools and educational experiences with microaggressions, prejudice, racism, and inequality can become internalized in conjunction with acculturative stress. This dynamic limits access to meaningful learning experiences. People who have experienced systemic marginalization to a marked degree are familiar with systemic oppression and marginalization. Therefore, some of the people with such experiences may also select psychological marginalization as a familiar and consistent coping strategy. This can also help to explain individual resistance to cultural responsiveness. Because another person has not been exposed to marginalization to a marked degree, they cannot internalize the value of cultural responsiveness.

## Evaluating Levels of Acculturative Stress

According to the American Psychological Association (APA, 2020), the assessment provides accurate and meaningful decision-making for specific outcomes. The word education is almost synonymous with the word evaluation. Various types of evaluations serve a variety of purposes. For this discussion, this section frames assessment as the quantification of acculturative stress, not academic assessment like summative or formative types. The assessment and measurement of acculturative stress are important because:

1. Research highlights the adverse effects on students' social-emotional and psychological well-being that directly impact learning outcomes.
2. Perceptions and realities of equity or the lack thereof threaten to the learning process.
3. Equity is often part of a larger narrative of inclusion. A measurement of the outcomes, when a lack of equity is perceived, is important in understanding practical applications of cultural responsiveness.
4. Educators desire a comprehensive system for applying cultural responsiveness to areas of planning, designing, and teaching.
5. Cultural responsiveness should be multifaceted and targeted to the psychological issue of marginalization, a construct that directly impacts one's ability to socialize, think, and perceive effectively.

The evaluation of acculturative stress consists of several key elements (see Appendix A). Effective identification and evaluation of acculturative stress are critical to understanding how culturally responsive practitioners employ the most effective techniques. Effective measures seem to be elusive.

The truth is, assessments are a given in the educational and psychological spaces but regularly fail to explore the role of variables that hold the key to effective culturally responsiveness. The overarching aim of evaluating acculturative stress is to better understand cultural responsiveness and its application in educational environments. This next will outline general assessment strategies that can assist with pinpointing acculturative stress.

## Measuring Marginalization and Acculturative Stress

Historically, acculturative stress and the four coping strategies have been applied topically throughout educational research. Measuring acculturative stress through culturally responsive evaluations can help us understand and apply more accurate techniques of cultural responsiveness. This includes teaching and design strategies and organizational climate. Prior to measuring acculturative stress, **informed consent is always required.**

We often assume individuals recognize and "manage" with their experiences with racism, prejudice, and oppression. Providing a formal evaluation of experiences documents and quantifies experiences that produce acculturative stress. A comprehensive evaluation supports efforts to address negative systemically pervasive experiences.

**Formal assessment** is an inquiry within the learning environment to obtain data through general methods of clinical means. According to the APA (2013) "testing and assessment allows a psychologist to see the full picture of a person's strengths and limitations" (Eabon & Abrahamson, 2013). Personal frameworks and experiences of researchers are cited as validity influencers (Alakhunova, 2015).

A formal assessment to measure acculturative stress levels in conjunction with marginalization and ethnic identity can help specify the appropriate cultural responses. A measure called the Multidimensional Acculturative Stress Inventory (MASI) (Rodriguez et al., 2002) is commonly used to measure levels of acculturative stress. As recently as 2020, increased numbers of researchers have validated the MASI (Scholaske, Rodriguez, Sari, Spallek, Ziegler, & Entringer). Therefore, the MASI would be considered a formal assessment of acculturative stress. This would help identify acculturative stress levels among individuals within a system that produces marginalization.

The MASI tool is a typical representation of assessing acculturative stress and its potential impact on the learning environment. The advantages of this type of assessment give insight into where the acculturative stress may impact students learning, socialization, and individual situations concerning their current circumstances and experiences with campus life. The MASI tool also fosters a reduction in researcher subjectivity.

In addition to the MASI (Rodriguez et al., 2002) Bashir and Khalid (2020) created a multi-dimensional Likert scale of 24 comprehensive questions to help identify levels of acculturative stress among those attending a post-secondary institution. This Acculturative Stress Scale for Pakistani Students (ASSPS) instrument created by Bashir and Khalid (2020) can help pinpoint acculturative stress and its origins. Some of the origins include academic, discrimination, cultural and religious origins. The MASI and the Bashir and Khalid (2020) survey tools can help clinical practitioners evaluate acculturative stress for educational support and learning outcomes. A sample formal assessment for acculturative stress is presented in Appendix A.

The inclusion of culturally responsive supports based on formal assessment may require significant restructuring of or additions to organizational structure to include professionals who can conduct such assessments and are well-versed in the appropriate academic and social supports required to support students with high levels of acculturative stress.

**Informal assessment** is an exercise conducted within the learning environment to obtain data through general methods of inquiry through general contact between students, peers, and/or co-workers. This method can be more qualitative but could result in some quantitative elements or data. For example, qualitative elements of informal assessment of acculturative stress may include general conversation, discussion posts, and one-on-one conversations. Quantitative examples may include looking at academic course metadata regarding interactions rates with specific course content. The advantages of data assessment include quick speed, personal (first-hand observations and anecdotes), and are easily applied for specific use in the classroom setting.

The disadvantages of informal assessment include a broad generalization and application of marginalization and acculturative stress factors. Potentially poorly worded or un-normed assessments could cause additional acculturative stress for individuals. Researchers suggest educators work from formal data collection and assessment types as well as clinical practitioners before applying informal data collection to inform course design and teaching practices.

Because formal and informal assessments have both advantages and disadvantages for the data collectors, clinicians, educators, co-workers, and students, a third option would be to consider a screening tool (informal assessment). General screening tools are easily added to institutional surveys. **General screening tools** can also be effective. A screening tool will allow some degree of reliability with room for culturally responsive practitioners and student service specialists to conduct a less formal inquiry with flexibility and meaning.

This is an assessment/survey constructed for general use, and although suggested, minimal clinical training is required. For example, a screening tool (Duffy et al., 2019) can highlight one aspect of a construct like marginalization. Combining a screening tool with a comprehensive understanding of how to implement culturally responsive interventions and other data points within lived experiences can provide meaningful information that supports inform decision-making about instruction, design, and organizational climate. Institutional data with a culturally responsive structure can improve organizational climate and student outcomes. Results guide and inform instructional designers, professors, administration, other staff, and/or students about lived experiences associated with higher education.

For the purposes of general health and wellness, reliable and identifiable levels of acculturative stress emerged only after an meaningful assessment. After talking with individuals and identifying the acculturative stress levels, personalized cultural responsiveness trends emerge. These trends help identify what culturally responsive intervention or accommodation is most appropriate for the learning process for a specific individual.

An evaluation of acculturative stress can present a specific psychological picture of what the student is experiencing and identifiable ways to support the student (see Appendix A). Data gained from such an evaluation can benefit the practitioner and student by providing recommendations for effective cultural responsiveness in the learning environment.

## Chaos To Clarity

Measuring acculturative stress helps identify the appropriate cultural responses that foster learning and meaningful cultural steps towards well-being. Yet, more questions have arisen that support the research imbalance:

- Are the current expectations of culturally responsive teaching methods focused on institutions, smaller departments, or individuals like educators, course designers, and students?
- Do institutions know or understand that a change has occurred, and do institutions desire the actual outcomes of culturally responsive teaching?
- What are the appropriate teaching and course design practices for best outcomes associated with cultural responsiveness?
- What type of documentation is acceptable or desired to support the use or implementation of culturally responsive teaching?

## What are the answers to these questions?

It's probable that answers to the questions above differ significantly among individuals and across institutions. For instance, one institution may provide culturally responsive professional development and have no way to support the application of such concepts. Or maybe, instructional designers and faculty members might be developing courses in a Universal Design for Learning (UDL) lens.

Although very useful in some instances and widely practiced, UDL often omits culturally specific considerations. General concepts regarding cultural responsiveness educators and instructional designers with a fairly nebulous approach to cultural responsiveness. It is likely the application of UDL decreases the cultural responsiveness required to overcome acculturative stress.

According to Yin (2010), one of the best ways to learn or model best practices is to use a case study model. In other words, working with each educator and student as an individual or a single subject or as it applies to specific courses. The following chapters present an evidenced-based process of cultural responsiveness.

An evidenced-based model of cultural responsiveness is beneficial. Later on, we will explore one such model. The process assists administration, educators, and designers implement and reach diversity, equity, and inclusion goals and outcomes for individuals who experience varying levels of acculturative stress. For now, be aware that a system exists to improve applicational for cultural responsiveness.

## Questions about cultural responsiveness and effectiveness

Human intersectionality and uniqueness among individuals are essential when discussing a systems approach.  An effective systems approach to cultural responsiveness supports whole group instruction, collaborative experiences, and recognizes individual variances. The following questions provide evidence for the difficulty in understanding applications of cultural responsiveness:

- Can cultural responsiveness support meaningful learning outcomes?
- Are culturally responsive teaching and design methods observable in the course design, curriculum, and instruction via meta-data?
- Are culturally responsive teaching and design methods universal?
- What are the specific practices associated with evidenced-based cultural practices?
- Was the student experiencing acculturative stress?  If so, what was done in the teaching and design process to reduce the stress of the learning experience?
- Are there observable and documentable cognitive, visual, and social cues within the teaching and course design that support the reduction of acculturative stress?

Such questions underscore the importance of effective and measurable needs and applications of cultural responsiveness. Thus, the most crucial role of culturally responsive course design or teaching methodology is a model is to support, measure, and document evidence-based cultural responses and interventions that reduce acculturative stress.

For example, educators may select or design a curriculum, yet they are unsure whether it reaches the level of cultural responsiveness required to reduce acculturative stress. A systems model for cultural responsiveness assists educators and instructional designers answer such questions. Alternatively, too much emphasis on cultural responsiveness and the frequency of such practices can negatively influence individual outcomes if applied inappropriately to one student or the whole class. This also highlights the need for a more robust model for applying cultural responsiveness.

## Putting It Together

Acculturative stress impacts individuals in unique ways. Individuals select responses to manage the levels of acculturative stress. This variance suggests cultural responses to acculturative stress likely fall within a bell curve. Outliers will also exist. Both facts support the need for more understanding of cultural responsiveness.

Culturally responsive design and instruction support better outcomes for learners. Instructional designers and instructional staff can decrease acculturative stress levels among individuals within the institution by considering the impact of cultural responses and the learning environment.

The measurement of acculturative stress provides insight into the effects of acculturative stress in the learning environment. The evaluation of acculturative stress also creates patterns of identifiable makers associated with teaching and design. These patterns fall into three groups: *whole group instruction, collaborative learning, and individual instruction.* These identifiable patterns provide a foundation for effective organization and implementation of cultural responsiveness in the classroom. In Chapter 4 a tiered system called the culturally responsive system (CRS) is introduced. The purpose of a culturally responsive system is to target general and specific cultural responses to acculturative stress.

## Chapter 3

## The Reasons for a Robust Framework of Cultural Responsiveness

According to Fraise & Brooks (2015), institutions make implicit and explicit assumptions about culture and its influence on teaching and learning practices. The assumptions are:

1.    Institutions are removed from general society and focus solely on the microcosm of the institutions.
2.    Institutions consistently disregard the social aspects of learning.
3.    Research propagated by institutions rejects (or discourages the acceptance of) the importance of personal and unique dynamics such as race, ethnicity, gender, and sexual orientation.
4.    "Diversity is detrimental to the work of a school since success is often defined as a normative construct framed through male whiteness"(Brookes, 2015, p. 7).
5.    "There is some kind of monolithic 'school culture' that means the same thing to all participants, rather than acknowledging that there are many cultures and sub-cultures flowing into and out of the school and that every individual interprets the significance of

these in a unique manner" (Brookes, 2015, p. 7).

Cultural responsiveness provides a mechanism that diminishes such assumptions, as outlined by Fraise and Brooks (2015). Cultural responsiveness is a tool to help re-shape the view of best practices as well as broader organizational strategy. As stated earlier in chapters, one of the difficulties with effectively applying culturally responsive strategies is the lack of a system that supports validity, reliability, and cohesiveness of practice. This absence of an evidenced-based application system places practitioners at a disadvantage when advocating for consistent application cultural responsiveness:

1.    It is hard to measure its effectiveness.
2.    Cultural responsiveness is considered an addition to educational space and not embedded best practice.
3.    Practitioners need to guess what is culturally responsive for a whole group, collaborative, and/or individual instruction.

The next chapter aims to introduce a system for applying cultural responsiveness to teaching and course design that helps practitioners and should answer the most common questions:

•    Which responsive strategies are the most effective?

- How do practitioners effectively apply cultural responsiveness when tied to desired outcomes?
- How do we effectively design, educate, introduce, and document our culturally responsive teaching and design efforts?
- How do we know what frequency, techniques, and design strategies work most effectively?
- When do practitioners stop one approach and start another?

## Point 1: Resistance and Process

Resistance can equal racism. Resistance to cultural responsiveness in education can also mean educators do not clearly understand what cultural responsiveness brings to a learning experience. For example, attributes of ethnic culture can motivate, engage, and help remediate students' academic issues and concerns when traditional methods seem to have failed. Additionally, cultural responsiveness can support the well-being of colleagues.

A uniformity among applications of cultural responsiveness is necessary. Educators need a more effective system to validate and document cultural responsiveness in spaces where cultural responsiveness' importance may be diminished or downplayed. Not having an effective scope of practice, creates pockets of resistance that are consistently reinforced within the environment.

## Point 2: Evidence-Based Practice

Also highlighted by Fraise & Brooks (2015), evidence-based practices have developed historically within the vacuum of a homogeneous research population. In addition, historical practices do not explore the concepts deep enough to construct alternative approaches that would be more effective with systematically marginalized individuals.

If the evidence-based practices are not appropriately constructed to meet the needs of systematically marginalized and racialized people, then in many cases, the system is propagating failure. In other words, a plane cannot fly without an engine. This is why cultural responsiveness is so important. And to revisit the metaphor, it is likely that the plane will not fly without the presence of a technician bringing available techniques, tools, and time.

## Point 3: Evidence-Based Barriers

Marginalization is a barrier to connectedness, socialization, and learning. Marginalization and acculturative stress occur socially and systemically. As explored earlier, an individual's self-selected ways of coping with the cultural differences in the environment might include marginalization. Unfortunately, the current evidence-based practices do not inherently address cultural barriers such as marginalization. In many instances, marginalization can impact individuals performance outcomes. There are also methods to design and teach through marginalization (as a response) to support the learning outcomes.

## Applications of Cultural Responsiveness

Cultural responsiveness has gained momentum across teaching and learning institutions in the United States. As a result, there is little need to revisit history or why the need for culturally responsiveness is relevant. However, it is essential to highlight the next steps of its application.

- Culturally responsiveness relies on an individual's level of desire and effectiveness at applying culturally responsive teaching practices in the classroom.
- Culturally responsiveness is a framework that supports the inclusion and application of cultural realities, norms, and variances within the teaching and learning process as well as organizational structure.
- Culturally responsive teaching requires an organized for design, planning, and application structure.
- Culturally responsive course design is growing in popularity, but it is still an emerging topic of research and theoretical development.

## Evidence-Based Frameworks and Concepts:

The following points support the need for an evidence-based framework for culturally responsive practices. Culture influences learning and the human experience. Learning psychology and educational practices are foundationally void of cultural considerations. Yet, many researchers do not cite culture as a limitation within the research studies (Fraise & Brooks, 2014). The current frameworks support general applications of cultural responsiveness. A more intentional approach is required to move the practice of cultural responsiveness to the forefront. The following quotes from the research are provided to highlight the culture and cultural responsiveness.

- Cultural psychology is "the study of the way cultural traditions and social practices regulate, express, transform, and permute the human psyche resulting in less psychic unity for humankind than in ethnic divergences in mind, self, and emotion" (Shweder, 1990, p. 1).
- "Culture is the deeply-learned confluence of language, values, beliefs, and behaviors that pervade every aspect of a person's life, and it is continually undergoing changes" (Geertz, 1973, p46).
- "Culture is dynamic and changing. It is not an isolated, mechanical aspect of life that can be used to explain phenomena in the classroom directly or that can be learned as a series of facts, physical elements, or exotic characteristics"

(Ovando, Collier, & Combs, 2003, p78).

- "Different aspects and dimensions of motivation, such as confidence, intellectual curiosity, attribution about past successes or failures, awards, punishments, materials, atmosphere, have been found out" (Altugan, 2015).
- Culture significantly impacts how students will respond in a classroom setting (Ginsburg, 2001).
- "Much attention has already been devoted to considering how cultural diversity may be accommodated in academic communities and how this may affect course design" (Hofstede, 1986; Sweeney, Weaven & Herington, 2008; Vatrapu & Suthers, 2007; Stepanyan et al., 2014, p. 676).
- "The pursuit for understanding interaction within and across cultural groups must be con-textualized within the studied educational environment. Learning activities and course structure can significantly alter the patterns and the levels of participant interaction. Earlier research concerning multicultural group work focuses on the challenges associated with communication skills, group composition, leadership, decision making and conflict management (Popov et al, 2012; Stepanyan et al., 2014, p. 676).

## Putting It Together

If you have a love of learning, you attend a lot

of professional development sessions. If you were to reflect on your professional development experiences, you likely have a variety of training remnants from workshops, webinars, and trainings that you have been to in the past. Worksheets, notes, notebooks, presentation slides, pamphlets, and the list of links you swore you would revisit before last semester but, still haven't quite gotten to it yet.

If you were going to organize your pd materials how would you do it? By the time-line (when you attended the workshops? By effectiveness?, Or maybe by personal preference? Maybe a type of professional needs assessment deciding what to keep and what to throw away because it is outdated? Would you start by throwing things away or just ignore the task?

What most of us dream of the organized professional development resource. But, few of us achieve "it". "It" refers the pot of gold at the end of the rainbow. In other words, the organized portfolio that outlines system of practices and acts as a professional reference to be used at a moment's notice. Similarly, an organized system of best practices would be beneficial when identifying and developing cultural responsiveness to instructional design and teaching practices.

The preceding points lead to a conclusion. While culturally responsive practices are applied in educational spaces, educators need a more robust process to support the practices within the educational system. Likewise, educators and instructional designers need functional support when applying cultural responsiveness within the larger educational system. The information provided in this chapter highlights the critical need for a formal process to help educators and instructional designers consistently apply effective CRS© techniques. The next chapter presents a model of effective applying cultural responsiveness.

# Chapter 4

## The Culturally Responsive System (CRS)© -
## Creating a Solid Foundation
## for Culturally Responsive Practice

Although models of cultural responsiveness exist within the research, few use psycho-cultural attributes to support effective learning (Ross, 1995). The Culturally Responsive Systems (CRS) model expands the current theoretical models of evidence-based practices. This problem-solving model is grounded in psycho-cultural learning theory. Using a problem-solving model, the tiered model illustrates the lack of cultural responsiveness in a learning environment. Each tier represents a strategy or approach to introducing culturally responsive practices within the classroom. Each tier comprises various techniques to help improve levels of cultural responsiveness in the classroom. The CRS model can also increase and become more or less responsive.

*Figure 4 - Culturally Responsive Teaching Model (Adapted from
RTI Model)*

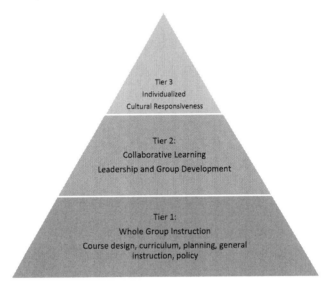

## Tier 1 - Whole Group Instruction

Instructional and design methods in Tier 1 can benefit all individuals. Tier 1 methods are generalized methods designed for individuals who require 0-20% percent of the learning environment to be culturally responsive. In most instances, this includes adjustments to planning, announcements, sense of community, course, and climate within the course ecosystem with very few instructional adjustments. It also may focus on more cultural competency rather than cultural responsiveness. UDL would be considered a tier 1 practice.

All individuals receive cultural responsiveness within whole group considerations. Tier provides opportunities for building cultural competency and decreasing cultural taxation. This occurs through increasing inclusion via course design, planning, and instruction, with little to some differentiation included. This also includes avenues to increase the cultural competency of students and instructors.

## Tier 2 - Collaboration and Group Development

Instructional and design methods in Tier 2 are for collaborative learning and group development. Tier 2's intermediate teaching methods are designed for students who require 20-50% percent of instruction to be culturally responsive and decrease acculturative stress to the level where learning can take place. This method includes a more specific emphasis on collaboration and group membership and development, interpersonal communication, and outcomes. All students receive culturally responsive teaching and/or support methods when working in small groups and collaborative learning experiences. A more specific focus on key components of cultural responsiveness that support students in collective learning experiences. Little to some differentiation is required in both Tiers 1 and 2.

## Tier 3 - Individualized Instruction or Course

## Design

Instructional and design methods in Tier 3 applied to a specific small group of individuals or an individual student. These cultural responses are most often used for individuals struggling to acclimate to environment or where levels of acculturative stress are present to a marked degree. Methods found in Tier 3 cultural responsiveness are designed for students who require 50% percent or more instruction to be culturally responsive to find academic success within their learning environment.

Tier 3 methods can be applied because the acculturative stress levels are so high that specific supports are required to support student learning outcomes. (See Appendix A). This Tier is for students who are assessed as experiencing acculturative stress. Tier 3's responses are specific to an individual student. This method includes instruction techniques, active learning, and an increase in divergent thinking.

*Figure 5 - Culturally Responsive Strategies (CRS)© Model*

| Cultural Responsiveness Teaching System and Process CRS© | | | |
|---|---|---|---|
| Cultural Response to Acculturative Stress | Assimilation | Integration | Separation | Marginalization |
| Cultural Responsiveness Required | Tier 1 | | Tier 2 | Tier 3 |

Best Practices Cultural Strategies, Responses, and Interventions

Everyone learns differently. The CRS provides culturally responsive practitioners with a roadmap to teaching and course design practices.   Some individuals understand concepts with ease, while others take more time to become proficient.  Other individuals prefer modalities and support structures to experience academic success.  The Tier system also responds to this reality (see figure 6).

*Figure 6 - Culturally Responsive Measurement Process*

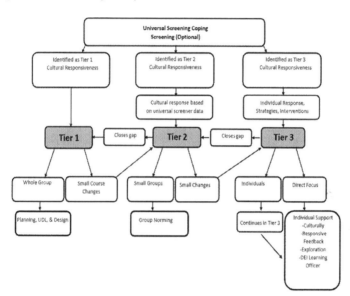

The CRS model fits within the foundations of the RTI model (NASP, 2021; Berkley et al.; 2020; Eagle et al., 2014; Fuchs et al., 2012) of evidence-based practices and learning interventions.  The RTI model "offers expertise at many levels, from system-

wide program design to specific assessment and
intervention efforts with individual students" (NASP,
2000, p.1).

The CRS© model uses Response to
Intervention (RTI) process framework as a
foundational model. The RTI is used to measure a
student's academic success, target reasons why that
success is not occurring, and change strategies
supports learners prior to a psychological evaluation
for a learning disability. However, there are some
fundamental differences between the RTI and the
CRS© model (see figure 7). The CRS model differs
significantly from the application, use, and strategies
associated with the RTI model of practice.

*Figure 7 - A Response to Intervention (RTI) and Cultural*
*Responsiveness Teaching System (CRS©) Comparison*

| RTI | CRS© |
|---|---|
| ✓ Used in K-12 Learning | ✓ Can be used in any teaching and learning experience regardless of age, modality or educational setting. |
| ✓ Requires teachers do collect statistical data. | ✓ Does not require the collection of statistical data, unless desired. |
| ✓ Targets specific academic deficits behaviors or lack of performance of individual students. | ✓ Targets psychological and cultural barriers that contribute to negative academic and social outcomes. |
| ✓ Results in a psychological evaluation for learning needs. | ✓ Does not result in a psychological evaluation for learning needs. |
| ✓ Foundations found in Eurocentric frameworks of psychology and what works in specific settings | ✓ Foundations found in cultural responsiveness, community psychology, counseling psychology, the community |

| RTI | CRS© |
|---|---|
| related to socio-economic class. | of inquiry theory self-identity theory, learning and cognition. |

## Who Benefits?

Everyone can benefit from the CRS model. Each Tier has specific benefits for individuals who experience varying levels of acculturative stress and may use marginalization to respond to that stress. There are a few instances where using the wrong strategy can increase acculturative stress, but no greater than the general stress and marginalization within Tier 3 students (see Figures 8 and 9).

## Understanding the Tiers

Each Tier aligns with elements of the 13 respective standards.

**Tier 1** instruction and design can benefit anyone even if the supports are geared towards specific ethnic and intersectional cultural norms, and omitted from **academic and community culture**. These responses are usually user-friendly strategies that people are familiar with and common in the teaching environment.

**Tier 2** instruction and design are applied to **collaborative culture,** learning and group settings. Tier 2 strategies target specific attributes of collaboration and include consideration for attributes like connectedness, belonging, inclusion, participation, team building, team membership, leadership, and task completion.

**Tier 3** is for specific needs of individuals  or small groups of individuals (from the same ethnic group, per group request) with specific cultural needs. These strategies would be used for individual. Tier 3 is associated with **cognitive culture.**

*In ALL instances, individuals who know the strategy and that strategy will be applied by request only.  These strategies are not done to students but rather for them because they understand and have had the appropriate exposure to the intervention prior to working with an instructor.*

These strategies are mostly used for remediation, explanation, memorization, and clarification of course content.  Tier 3 methods are created based on evaluation results.  Similarly, to disability accommodations, Tier 3 strategies should not be used without the appropriate training. Culturally responsive clinical evaluations should only be completed by individuals with the appropriate training and credentials.  Check with your jurisdiction for details.
See uscaseps.org for more information.

*Figure 8 - Cultural Responsiveness Teaching System (CRS©)*

| CRS© Applications | | | |
|---|---|---|---|
| Tier | Tier 1 | Tier 2 | Tier 3 |
| What type of application? | Requires minimal CR | Require substantial CR | Requires very substantial CR |

Ethnic Culture and Intersectional Culture

The next table is a general overview of who is involved in this culturally responsive practice. The following chart helps to answer basic questions associated with this model. Individuals at the beginning stages of learning about cultural responsiveness often have questions about applying cultural responsiveness. To that end, the following chart was developed to support answering such questions.

*Figure 9 - The Frequently Asked Applications Chart*

| CRS© Applications | | | |
|---|---|---|---|
| | Tier 1 | Tier 2 | Tier 3 |
| | All individuals | Small Groups - ***Not ethnic small groupings*** | Individual – or – groups of less than 5 students |
| **Who is involved?** | Instructional Designers, Practitioners, and students, LODEIs | LODEIs, Practitioners and Students | Practitioners and Students and/or LODEIs |

| CRS© Applications | | | |
|---|---|---|---|
| | **Tier 1** | **Tier 2** | **Tier 3** |
| **What's the Purpose?** | To add up to 20% of cultural responsiveness to a course | To add between 20-50% of cultural responsiveness to a course | To surpass 50% of cultural responsiveness to a course |
| **How will it happen?** | Course design, course set-up, student contribution, and instruction | Curriculum selection options, robust reflection, Culturally Responsive Taxonomy for Learning | Culturally responsive feedback, culturally responsive specialized supports. |

Tiers align with standards of practice, but each tier also aligns with the different types of cultures found in the ACCCE model of culture (academic, community, collaborative, cognitive, and ethnic/intersectionality culture). Educators should use considerations of culture and the tiers to support cultural responsiveness within their scope of practice. Figure 10 presents the ACCCE model with three tiers of cultural responsiveness.

*Figure 10 - Academic Culture and Tier Learning*

| **Types of Culture** | **TIER 1 Academic and Community** | **TIER 2 Collaborative** | **TIER 3 Cognitive** |
|---|---|---|---|
| Academic Collaborative Community Cognitive *Ethnic* & *Intersectionality* *(ACCCE)* *(All Tiers)* | **Academic culture:** Belongingness, inclusion, equity, self-identity. (Planning, Announcements, Content, Policy) | Group forming and norming, participation, outcomes, interpersonal communication, and socialization. (Collaboration- | This includes, decision making, emotions, impressions, perception, and attention, cognition. (Instruction/Active Learning/Divergent |

| Types of Culture | TIER 1 Academic and Community | TIER 2 Collaborative | TIER 3 Cognitive |
|---|---|---|---|
| | **Community culture:** learners as stakeholders, decision makers, and care takers. (Sense of Community, Climate, and Course Ecosystem) | Group Membership) | Thinking) |
| **Which individuals?** | All students in the whole group | Each student within the small group. | Individual students or small groups requiring specific CR. |

Selecting an evidence-based practice for course design and teaching can seem overwhelming because it differs significantly from the frequently referenced frameworks. The inability to organize, document, or quantify the effectiveness of such efforts has been hampered until now. Applying the CRS model establishes a foundation for educators and designers to do more than just surface-level teaching and course design.

## Putting It Together

This chapter presented the next logical and equitable step for cultural responsiveness. An effective system for evaluating, decision-making, planning, and designing for culturally responsive learning experiences responding to acculturative stress is necessary and warranted.

Historically, educators and instructional designers applied the same techniques and have not changed the of students' academic outcomes experiencing high levels of acculturative stress. Cultural responsiveness applied as a problem-solving tool to support learning gains has yet to occur in U.S. educational institutions. Thus, the need to focus on acculturative stress developed outside and within institutions as the problem, with appropriate cultural responses as a solution, and a working and tenable intervention to increase individual well-being.

# Chapter 5

## Case Studies and Examples

Examples in action always help illustrate the use of any practice. The following chapter presents case studies for application and practice of the CRS model.

## The Student and Culturally Responsive Practitioner

*Mark, a 21-year-old African American male, is attending an introductory STEM course at his local university. His past experiences in school have been average at best, but he is determined to succeed on his higher education journey. He was nervous about attending the first day of his STEM course. When Mark entered the classroom, he found a place to sit and waits for the course to begin. Prior to his STEM course, Mark attended his culturally responsive, college success course. Mark and his peers were offered an optional acculturative stress scale as part of that course. The scale was offered after a lesson in acculturative stress and cultural responsiveness. This was an optional lecture and activity. If desired, individuals could share their findings from their scales. The instructor also collaborated with the campus counselor to offer additional guidance and support.*

*The instructor explained that students would benefit from culturally responsive teaching methods and traditional teaching methods. This is because the instructor privately reviewed the student scores prior to submission. Most students in the class scored within scored an 80% or above on acculturative stress levels.*

*The instructor worked with the course designer to design culturally responsive course elements. The course designer, a certified Learning and Online Diversity, Equity, and Inclusion Officer© CASEPS, designed a course to address the high levels of acculturative stress.*

*The instructor then gave Mark and his peers time to collaborate and find aspects of the class they felt were culturally responsive. Mark and his partner, Hadassah, found three areas: 1) A welcome message supporting the importance of diversity, equity, and inclusion that went beyond the cut and paste of the university's diversity statement (Tier 1), 2) a cultural lab and collaborative outline of the role of culture and collaboration (Tier 2), and 3) an opportunity to have culturally responsive*

*feedback if students are struggling to*
*understand a concept (Tier 3).*

From Mark and Hadassah's perspective, the Tiers are irrelevant. For practitioners and instructional designers, it helps pinpoint the course's appropriate design and instructional methods.

*Figure 11 - Examples of Tier 1 Cultural Responsiveness*

| Learning and Cognition | Socialization |
|---|---|
| • A culturally responsive introduction question. | • A general announcement about the importance of DEIA. |
| • Identify communal academic resources and their uses. | • Cultural norms of the environment are established. |
| • Create cultural competency goals for one or two assignments or outcomes. | • Create a sense of community rubric. |

*Figure 12 - Examples of Tier 2 Cultural Responsiveness*

| Learning and Cognition | Socialization |
|---|---|
| • Culturally responsive learning labs. *How did erosion effect different ethnic groups in different places?* | • Create a safe space within your LMS. Make spaces for difficult conversations. |
| • Identify communal academic resources and cultural impacts of such resources. | • Have students help develop collaborative norms for active or group learning. |
| • Create interdependent learning goals for collaborative assignments. | • Provide various opportunities to connect with outside resources that are reflective of the diversity among the student population. |

*Figure 13 - Examples of Tier 3 Cultural Responsiveness*

| Learning and Cognition | Socialization |
|---|---|
| • Introduce complex story telling. | • Provide time for students to psychologically suite themselves in group setting. Provide pre-collaborative supports about cultural differences in groups dynamics. |
| • Interwoven competency based on lived experiences. | • Foster exploration of self-identity in relationship with concepts taught. |
| • Identify specific strengths and their relationship to specific realities.<br>• Increase opportunities for divergent thinking. | • Engage with a LODEI to decrease marginalization of online spaces. |

## Instructional Designer Case Study

*Kala is a 30-year-old instructional designer at a public college located in an urban area. She wants to develop culturally responsive courses. The CRS methodology is a new concept for her, and she feels overwhelmed by re-developing old courses from scratch and designing new courses.*

*When she reviewed her CRS© training, she realized the various ways to implement the cultural responsiveness. Her first option is to 1) identify courses that hadn't yet been designed. Her second option is to work with courses in specific content areas. Kala's third option is to work with a faculty member who holds CASEPS culturally responsive teaching certification or DEI Officer of Learning Certification. Since this model is new to Kala and she is looking for support, she selected option 3.*

*Kala and her co-worker Jung worked together with Maria, the LODEI, to identify the areas to implement cultural responsiveness. The Department of Institutional Effectiveness results suggested that many of the students require a Tier 3 level of course design at this time. Kala and her co-workers are up for the challenge. First, they review the comparison of traditional and culturally responsive course design (See Figure 14).*

*Figure 14 - Comparison of Culturally Responsive Design*

| Categories | Instructional Design | Culturally Responsive Course Design |
|---|---|---|
| **Instructional Model** | Bloom's Taxonomy (1956) Kolb's (1976) | Culturally Responsive Taxonomy Kolb's Revised |
| **Learning Styles** | Kinesthetic, Visual, | Familiarity with culture, academic, ethnic, collaborative. |
| **Model of Objectives** | Independent Learning Goals Competency Based Learning Goals | Collaborative, Interdepend, and Altruistic Learning Goals |
| **Content** | Discuss, explore, explain. | Revisit the past, link learning to specific cultural relevancy and responsiveness. |
| **Academic Assessment** | Multiple choice and written assignment. | Group presentations, collective assessment, and oral examination |

| Categories | Instructional Design | Culturally Responsive Course Design |
|---|---|---|
| | | (live or recorded). Cultural lens approach to assessment (Hardin et al., 2014; Trandias, 1996) |
| **Agency** | Increase agency through skills building. | Increase agency through lived experiences and cultural relevancy. |
| **Deliverables** | Options based on learning preferences (Bloom's Taxonomy). | Options based on culturally responsive learning preferences (Campbell-Whatley, 2015). |
| **DEI** | General statement about DEI. | Embedding DEI practices throughout the course. |

After their review, they decided to focus on an introductory writing course since the institutional data supports the need for high cultural responsiveness in those courses. Kala and her team created the following changes to the course to address the lack of cultural responsiveness (see Figure 15).

*Figure 15 - Planning for Course Changes*

| Planning | | |
|---|---|---|
| | *Current Design* | *Culturally Responsive Design Changes* |
| ***General Changes to the Course*** | *Course Introduction* | • *Added statement on the importance of culturally responsive teaching.* |
| | *Assessment* | • *Created a culturally responsive rubrics have been developed and added to the course based on student* |

| | | |
|---|---|---|
| | | demographics. |
| DEI | | • Added a sense of community rubric to the course and added goals and objectives about sense of community. |
| Agency | | • Changed language from student to academic stakeholders. |

Then Kala and co-workers decided to make the following changes to increase cultural responsiveness in the design process.

*Week Four:*

*Current Course Assignment - For this group writing assignment, you should begin pre-writing by listing problems on campus that your group has identified and that could have realistic solutions. After narrowing down your list to two or three issues, discuss the issues and assess which issues could potentially be solved.*
*Consider the university as your audience. Working as a team of six, you will each be responsible for doing the basic research, surveys, or interviews with your peers on campus to create a proposal to the university. Keep in mind that the proposal must be suited to the appropriate university department, board, or administrative office that oversees the issue. Length: 6-8 pages (each team member will be responsible for doing the footwork on the proposal, writing one major section of the proposal, and revisions.)*

*Culturally Responsive Design Change* - *This week is a group writing assignment. Prior to working in groups, students are to explore what they value most in a group by taking the group preference survey. This will allow you and your team members to explore what is important to you when working in groups. Once you have completed the anonymous survey, the results will be shared with the class. Students will then be assigned to groups, and you will share what is important to you about working in a group and why. The teams will then make team charters based on those norms. Then the directions will follow.*

*Week 12 -*

*Current Course Assignment* - *Culminating Activity, Individual 12-page Essay*

*Culturally Responsive Design Change* –*Students will write an essay that reflects or represents someone close or a topic of their choice OR discuss how the cultural use of writing differs from what was learned in the course. Students will then reflect, compare, and contrast class culture with peers.*

## Faculty Case Studies

## Educator Case Study 1:

*Ng is a faculty member of color who works at a predominately white institution. He is experiencing acculturative stress within his institution and struggling to connect with his mostly white student population. He is more familiar with Chinese culture. He completed the training in culturally responsive teaching and CRS©. He wants to develop culturally responsive courses. Although this is a new concept for him, he feels overwhelmed by re-developing old courses and designing new courses.*

*Ng decided to take the trainer's advice and implement one of the best practices – 'start small.' Ng reviewed the aspects of European white cultural norms that align with teaching and learning practice that included, but was not limited to, English, Dutch, French, French Canadian, German, Finnish, and Swedish. His plan of action was the following (see Figure 16):*

*Figure 16 - Ng's Small Changes*

| Socialization | Grading | Collaboration Activity |
|---|---|---|
| **Week 1:** | **Week 4:** | **Week 7:** |
| *Ask a culturally responsive instruction question. (Tier 1)* | *Use culturally responsive grading and feedback when necessary. (Tier 3)* | *Allow for individualism within the collaboration as well as group identity. (Tier 2)* |

## Educator Case Study 2:

*Eric is teaching sociology and has been using the CRS© for five years. He is CRS©*

*Level 3 certified and also trains institutions on
how to implement CRS© strategies. Eric's
institution implemented CRS© across all
campuses. The instructional designers at
Eric's campus have designed course shells
using Tiers 1, 2, and 3.*

*Each class/individual is given a Tier score
based on the students' average scores within
the class. The Tier score is based on a survey
given to incoming students. That data is
collected and added to the student portal to
provide Eric with more information about how
he may help each student.*

*The completion of the survey results in a
score for Tier 1, 2, or 3 practices designation.
Eric can then adjust the course as needed or
request a specific level of cultural
responsiveness based on his students'
average scores from the LEMS (Duffy et al.,
2019).*

*When Eric logs into his course shell, he is
given specific information to support his
students. For instance, when Eric logs into his
learning management system, his student
roster has important information associated
with each student:*

**Roster Example:**
Class score: 1.5 (Tier 1)
Jane Doe (she/they) Tier 2

*Because students may not know what cultural responsiveness is, Eric's university has set up options for culturally responsive college success courses and culturally responsive education courses that are designated electives.*

*As a side note, Eric mentions, culturally responsive electives support student learning. Students are given a brief introduction to culturally responsive teaching, samples of what it would look like, and time to discuss with peers or decide if this is needed. Courses can also be provided through student services departments (multicultural clubs, etc.). With permission and informed consent, relevant data is then collected. When the student data is loaded to a course, instructors and designers have that information in the student's profile. The same culturally responsive samples given to students are introduced in the student orientation or college success course and officially approved for use.*

## Profile Example A:

*Student Name (his/her/them pronouns)*
*Tier: 1 (0-20%)*
*Request to Apply CRT: Yes*

## Profile Example B:

*Student Name (his/her/them pronouns)*
*Tier: 3 (50+%)*
*Request to Apply CRT: No*

> *This is the example that Eric gives to his peers who struggle to understand the process.*
> *Additionally, each Tier is associated with specific strategies, so Eric's peers do not have to start from a place of resistance.*

### Tier 2: Collaborative Case Study

> *Ishmael is a seasoned professor who recently completed his CASEPS certification for culturally responsive teaching. He is now ready to apply what he learned from his training in his learning environment. After reviewing institutional demographics, he realized that his institution has a predominately white student population. Yet, there are also students familiar with dual cultures, including African (various) Chinese-American, Pakistani-American, and Indigenous students attending his college. Ishmael knows from his training that:*

- **African Immigrant Cultural Group Development:** Africans' identities are found within the community's identity; community values often include values of harmony, cooperation, and communal attributes of social behavior.

- **Chinese Culture Group Development:** Observable correction of team members when necessary
- **Native American /First Nations Group Development:** Listening is a value and is essential to group norming.

*Ishmael uses that data to support cultural responsiveness in his class. For collaborative purposes, Ishmael understands that some students may require the reflection of their own identity within the course within various cultural frameworks. Ishmael creates a poll zoom.*

*Unlike a Tier 1 poll that would place random attributes to reflect different cultures, Ismael uses a Tier 2 method that targets the population's systemically-marginalized student populations and adds other cultural attributes of collaborative learning.*

*Ishmael did not place the cultural groups next to the correlating descriptor. Only he is aware of that.*

*On the first day of class, Ismael noticed that his student demographic was almost 100% White. He used the same poll anyway to place students in groups. At the end of the course, he shared a lesson in cultural responsiveness and shared that people are more alike than different and that culture is something of which everyone can be proud. He then shared the cultural attributes of his culture, Chinese culture.*

Figure 17 - Sample Poll for Students

| Add a Poll |
|---|
| Collaborative Response Question |
| 1.    What is most important to you when working in a group? <br>     ☒ Single Choice   ☐ Multiple Choice <br> ☐ Harmony <br> ☐ Clear Objectives <br> ☐ Understanding of User Experience <br> ☐ Listening and Storytelling <br> ☐ Extended Social Greetings <br> ☐ Observable Correction <br> ☐ Answer 7 (Other Optional Answers) |
| *Polling can be Completed via Mentimeter, Zoom, text messaging, or Textpolleverywhere* |

Although, Ishmael started to use a Tier 2 response, he ended up applying a Tier 1 response cultural response because it was based on multicultural education and building cultural competency, not a focusing on the betterment of small group collaboration. Students remained anonymous. Sharing the cultural diversity as it relates to collaborative learning of the answer selections was more of a teachable moment in cultural competency rather than cultural responsiveness.

## Tier 3 Case Study: Culturally Responsive Feedback (Tier 3 Response)

*Debbie is a White instructor working at a Historically Back College (HBCU). She is very active in causes of social justice and systemic reform. She has completed and reviewed her CRS© training in culturally responsive grading practices. Debbie asked her students to complete the LEMS (Duffy et al., 2019). It was an optional assignment.*

*Although Debbie's students attend an HBCU, Debbie found that 30% of her students reported high levels of marginalization in the learning space. Debbie decided to briefly discuss the findings with her campus LODEI. After talking with her students and consulting with her campus LODEI, Debbie offered students the opportunity to apply culturally responsive feedback to their papers.*

*Debbie showed the students examples of culturally responsive feedback. She told students it was an option to support them in their learning, and other grading and feedback methods could be used in conjunction with the culturally responsive feedback. Four of the students emailed Debbie later that week to express interest in the culturally responsive feedback. Debbie agreed to apply culturally responsive grading practices for the next assignment per the request of her students and with their informed consent.*

*In the meantime, Debbie reviewed other models of academic feedback. In preparing to apply culturally responsive feedback for Debbie's four students, she reviewed feedback samples used in the past for her writing assignment.*

*She now realizes that model of feedback was culturally responsive to European culture. Four European cultural groups were identified: Irish, English, German, and Dutch. Debbie thought this could be why her students were not reading or applying her feedback in the past. The sample model and what Debbie found are presented below.*

## Debbie's Academic Feedback

*"Thanks for submitting your essay - I enjoyed reading it. I hope my comments help you in your revision process. Your narrative is, without a doubt, at its best when you give vivid details of the day from your perspective, which is, as you describe, a unique one. The "chalky taste" of the air, for instance, is a detail that brings the scene to life.*

*You asked for help with structure, and I think the most sensible structure, in this case, is a chronological one. It's fine to start with a vivid scene to land the reader in the event, but then it makes sense to step back and tell the story as it happened. To help you accomplish this end, you might consider listing the major points you want to cover and then turning them into an outline. It might help, too, to think about the overall message you want to convey. Then make sure all of your details contribute to that message. As for constructive comments, you never really explain why you were at Ground Zero on September 12. Do you happen to live nearby? Did you have any special connection to the firefighters or the victims? Why did you decide to help out? I would also be careful of the very general statements you use to sum up the essay, such as, "That day brought to my attention a side of humanity that had lay dormant in my mind. That moment in time showed me that people have the capacity to act unselfishly." It's best to convey your point through examples rather than summation – the old advice to "show, not tell." It takes a lot of courage to tackle the events of September 11 and in the days following in an essay, but I think you have a great perspective and the ability to look beyond the chaos to the details of the scene." Feel free to write back as you revise this piece. I'd be glad to talk more about it.* - Retrieved from the Connors Family Learning Center www.bc.edu.

*First, Debbie notices the feedback sample she was given to follow was reflective of various European cultural values of grading, which include:*

### English (E)
- *consultative facilitation*
- *self-reflective*

### Dutch (D)
- *A focus on what is 'right'*

### German (G)
- *A balance of empathy and educational leadership:
  More leadership than empathy*

### Irish (I)
- *Importance of individual contributions.*

**Below is Debbie's feedback with the identifiable
cultural associations from the feedback example
provided above.**

- "Thanks for submitting your essay-I enjoyed
  reading it. (D) *The "right" behavior was to submit
  the essay.*
- I hope my comments help you in your revision
  process. (G) *A balance of empathy and
  educational leadership: More leadership than
  empathy*
- Your personal narrative is without a doubt at its
  best when you give vivid details of the day from
  your perspective, which is, as you describe, a very
  unique one. (I) *Importance of individual
  contributions*
- The 'chalky taste' of the air, for instance, is a detail

that really brings the scene to life. (I) *Importance of individual contributions*

- You asked for help with structure, and I think the most sensible structure in this case is a chronological one. *(E) Consultative Facilitation.*
- It's fine to start with a vivid scene to land the reader in the event, but then it makes sense to step back and tell the story as it happened. (E) *Consultative Facilitation*
- To help you accomplish this end, you might consider listing each of the major points you want to cover and then turning them into an outline. (E) *Consultative Facilitation*
- It might help, too, to think about the overall message you want to convey. (E) *Consultative Facilitation*
- Then make sure all of your details contribute to that message. As for constructive comments, you never really explain why you were at Ground Zero on September 12. (E) *Consultative Facilitation*
- Do you just happen to live nearby? Did you have any special connection to the firefighters or the victims? Why did you decide to help out? *(E) Self-reflective with Direct Questions instead of Open-ended*
- I would also be careful of the very general statements you use to sum up the essay, such as, "That day brought to my attention a side of humanity that had lay dormant in my mind. *(E) Consultative Facilitation*
- That moment in time showed me that people have

the capacity to act unselfishly." It's best to convey your point through examples rather than summation-the old advice to "show not tell." *(I) Individual Contributions*

- It takes a lot of courage to tackle in an essay the events of September 11 and the days following, but I think you have a great perspective and the ability to look beyond the chaos to the details of the scene." (D) *The right behavior was to submit the essay.*
- Feel free to write back as you revise this piece. I'd be glad to talk more about it. *(I) Importance of Individual Contributions*

*Debbie decided to take the notes she made above about the feedback and rewrite it for a Tier 3 Level of cultural responsiveness. She also met with her campus LODEI prior to working with her students. The LODEI also worked with the students prior to the feedback implementation. Her level of cultural responsiveness applied African American attributes of cultural responsiveness to the feedback:*

### *African American Culture*
- *Strength-Based Perspectives (SBP)*
- *Narratives (N)*
- *Collectivism(C)*
- *Communication and Highlighting of Specific Realities Both Historical and Present (CHSR)*

## Cultural Responsiveness Framework

## Engagement

*I am glad you exercised your ability to use your autonomy and explored a different method to assist you in your learning (SBP).*

- *The cultural and ethnic lens can be a powerful tool in understanding new content. (SBP)*
- *What you contributed to the learning this week demonstrates an authenticity that was not present in your last assignment. (SBP)*
- *Focusing on the content through your own cultural lens helped to minimize personally irrelevant aspects of the learning process and helped you make meaning of the content for yourself to align with your worldview. (SBP)*
- *Many of your peers also asked for help with structure. I will have to look at other ways to help us grow in this area as a community (C)*
- *These are some of the answers I have given on other papers to help for clarity. (C; CHRS)*
- *You started with a vivid scene. Storytelling is important to understand the reasons for how things originate and how they have evolved. In so many cultures, storytelling is central to the community. Try to explain then elements of your scene impacted on different levels. Did African American firefighters or rescue workers of color have other methods of coping with the*

*aftermath? That would help complete the narrative and give a more holistic picture of the events. (N; CHSR)*

- *It helps to make a video recording with the video on or off or record yourself talking out your main points. Listen to yourself and see if it makes sense or you need more organization in your thought. Some of my students have had friends and family listen to their outline for clarity or just have a conversation and use those main points to frame your writing outline. (N; SBP)*
- *Is that more of the message you would like to convey? (SBP)*
- *There are so many layers of who was involved and why it happened. I am listening to your story, but I have questions. If you were passing this story to your grandchildren, what details would you want them to know about why you were there or the circumstance that brought you there? Historical records for African American's are often incomplete. Writing a robust narrative is part of making a robust record of accurate events. You are part of the new history (N; CHSP)*
- *Again, for the historical record, verbiage like 'sum up' may change in the future. I want to continue to learn about your story and want to continue telling the story by being as clear and concise as possible. This is important to the accuracy of storytelling. Such as "Who I was*

*the day before, changed on that day. What else would you want people to know about your life prior to and afterwards? (N)*

- *Storytelling is significant and historical part of African and African American heritage. It belongs in the cultural framework of education. This story gives an excellent perspective through a cultural viewpoint and a unique lens that only you can provide. (SBP) Thank you for sharing it with me.*

Debbie applied an evidenced-based African-American cultural responsiveness to academic feedback. She is now ready to grade her student's next assignment with more relevant feedback to her students. With a few topic changes, this could be applied to multiple students. It is also important to re-emphasize those tier 3 interventions with the student's knowledge and understanding of the intervention. This type of feedback should never be completed without the student's understanding, informed consent, and/or request prior to implementation.

## Divergent vs. Convergent Thinking and Learning (Tier 3 Response)

According to Garrison et al. (2010), a revision of the COI presence model revealed that too much emphasis was placed on cognitive presence (critical thinking). This viewpoint is not surprising considering the cultural lens applied to the theory. Garrison and his colleagues (2010) are three white men who are most likely familiar with Eurocentric education norms, including clear assignment objectives, convergent thinking, and contractual understanding.

Divergent thinking is more common and recognized in many communal cultures, unlike convergent thinking associated with Eurocentric cultures. Some communal cultural norms support divergent thinking prior to critical thinking. What is divergent thinking? Divergent thinking is a type of thinking that easily aligns with cultural norms. Divergent thinking connects students' prior knowledge and cultural framework to the curriculum. Divergent thinking prompts questions such as: Why are these facts important to me?

If students are unable to answer the 'what facts are important to them' question, a pathway for experiences with marginalization and separation will grow. When students can answer that question and engage within the cultural context, it becomes easier to understand the instructor's curriculum and concepts. Examples are noted below:

- First-Nation Citizens/Native Americans – Interwoven competencies based on storytelling and metaphors prior to convergent thinking.
- Armenian Culture – Competency builds through adaptive practice.
- Italian Culture – Establish personal perspectives prior to divergent thinking.

Developing divergent thinking through cultural responsiveness can significantly impact learning outcomes. Culture is a motivating factor that supports further exploration and interest through relevant perceptions, attention, cognition, and emotion. Divergent thinking is applied as a cultural response in three ways: (1) inquiry, (2) instruction, and (3) active learning.

*Hugo is an instructional design working at an HSI. He has recently completed his LODEI© certification training and wants to focus on increasing the representation of divergent thinking across courses. He reviews his courses and decides to make a handout to help generalize the concepts of divergent thinking. Hugo understands that he does not have the ability to control decisions about providing culturally responsive evaluations at his campus. Hugo also knows that, divergent thinking diminished the application of marginalizing as a coping strategy. So, he decides to focus on professional development for his staff. He decides to highlight the following points:*

- *Divergent thinking is associated more with collectivists cultural.*
- *Divergent thinking draws out ideas that lead to facts.*
- *Divergent thinking also includes opportunities for elaboration and exploration.*

- *Divergent thinking supports multiple answers, that lead to a specific answer.*

## Case Study 4: Instructional Cultural Responsiveness and Divergent Thinking

*Xochitl (Sow-Cheel) teaches at a predominately white institution. Xochitl was born in Mexico and named after her grandmother but was raised in Columbia by her parents. She is more familiar with Colombian culture but has recently begun exploring her Mexican heritage. In the past, she has discussed the challenges of being a Latina familiar with Columbian heritage and the disappointment when people learn she is not as familiar with her Mexican heritage as her Columbian heritage. Xochitl works in a predominately white institution with her supervisor Margo. Margo calls Xochitl "Zoe," which she despises, because that is not her name. Xochitl repeatedly corrects Margo that her name is Xochitl pronounced (Sow-cheel). Xochitl reports this is one of the most unnecessarily taxing parts of her job. Xochitl also pointed out that she struggles to understand her students' behaviors and responses in class and the lack of connection she feels with some of her colleagues. Xochitl admits the racism is microaggression and is blatant, and other times less so. Xochitl, has addressed her concerns with the DEI officer on campus and some of her experiences are being investigated. Which only adds to Xochitl's desire to address this issue once and for all and at least with her students and maybe also in her working environment.*

*Xochitl shares that she understands she is not asking for racism or microaggressions to occur, but she recognizes that and wants a better way to cope with the stress it is causing her, while her campus DEI officer is looking into such matters. Xochitl sometimes feels marginalized by what she refers to as a "lack of understanding" specifically from her students about her experiences in the classroom. She states that she cannot hide the fact she is Latina. This creates a burden to answer student questions that sometimes are rude or uncomfortable to answer. She also notes that white instructors did not have the same challenges with their students. Xochitl is aware that such questions are not posed to her white colleagues, and it is because she is a visible minority, and that is why these unavoidable comments are made. The department dean suggested professional development on the CRS© model may be helpful.*

*After attending the training, Xochitl clarified why she struggled to connect with her students and some of her peers. Some students were not showing respect due to bias and/or racism.*

*This was very clear. Xochitl could also see where some students relied on academic and cultural norms to navigate the learning environment. Xochitl recognized that she was attempting to teach in a way that did not reflect her own culture. She learned aspects of Eurocentric culture directly conflicted with her own and impact her teaching process. Xochitl compared Applied Columbian Culture and Applied European culture and learning.*

*Figure 18 - Columbian vs. Eurocentric (Plotts, 2020a)*

| Columbian | Eurocentric |
|---|---|
| Columbian Cultural Lens: Skill Building and Application | Self-Reliant Skill Building (Scandinavian) |
| Columbian Cultural Lens: Students perceive investment in personal skill building as a caring act. | Independent and Acknowledgement of Pride (Slavic Czech) |
| Columbian Cultural Lens: Family loyalty is paramount. | Hospitality is paramount (Slavic Czech) |
| Columbian Cultural Lens: Significant access to medical care and extended resources when compared to their counterparts. | Self- Reliance (English Culture) |
| Columbian Cultural Lens: The feedback should reflect the cultural value of education and resourcefulness. | Consultative Facilitation (English) |
| Columbian Cultural Lens: Strong and consistent negotiation skills are a tool used to navigate collaborative experiences. | Practical Solutions (French Canadian) |

*Xochitl reported that understanding the different cultural responses and frameworks of her students and peers provided some clarity, but did not negate her other past experiences. After the training Xochitl, felt a better sense of well-being for two reasons: one because her experiences with racism and microaggressions were amplified by other faculty of color and she did not feel alone in her experiences, and two because Xochitl gained a better understanding of how her culture significantly contributed to the learning environment. Xochitl noted her favorite part of her professional development was Columbian culture was affirmed within the learning practices. Xochitl also reported this insight would not change the blatant racism and microaggression of students or peers. Xochitl hopes to learn more about how her Mexican cultural heritage can influence cultural responsiveness in her classroom.*

*The new insight can help Xochitl manage the acculturative stress in the environment more effectively and create healthy boundaries and outcomes for herself. This insight won't make her peers change their attitudes or behaviors. Xochitl's experience focused on her health and wellness.*

*Xochitl is now able to explore the differences in culture. Lastly, Xochitl also noted that although the training provided explanations and clarity, it does not excuse the*

*continuation of racism and microaggressions in
her workplace.  She will be looking for more
alternatives to address the continued
microaggressions from her supervisor.*

## Case Study 4b Instructional Cultural Responsiveness and Divergent Thinking in The Classroom

*It has been three months since Xochitl has
explored cultural responsiveness.  She is
preparing her classes for fall and wants to
focus on creating divergent thinking in her
courses.  Xochitl referred to her training
resources for help.  She remembered three
examples used in the course.*

### *Cultural examples of divergent thinking:*

- *Learning Through Metaphors (Many First
Nation Cultures)*
- *Perceptions About the Content (French
Canadian Culture)*
- *Personal Connection to The Content (Russian-
Jewish Culture)*

*Xochitl wanted to employ Tier 3 strategies
within the course.  Her lecture topic was*
Introduction to Organizational Leadership.  *She
wants to create a foundation to explore the
concepts of* problem-solving *and* strategic

thinking. *She applied each of these cultures to the learning process.*

*Xochitl knows most of her students are white and somewhat familiar with the academic culture and European cultural norms; she added other aspects of culture. The cultural viewpoints could be a foundation for culturally responsive scaffolding for other topics.*

*Below are Xochitl's prompts for divergent thinking and instruction:*

**Introduction to Organizational Leadership**

**Week 1 Lecture Launch (LL) and Assignment (A)**

**LL:** It is your first day on the job. An organizational leader says to all new people hired: "Here at X company, the world is your stage!" What does that mean to you? What message does that convey? To which symbology or metaphor might you respond? Example; "He has a heart of gold."

*The lecture will then explore various aspects of leadership and the various cultural implications. This concept will be tied with organizational leadership ethics and best practices.*

**A:** Assignment Option 1 Write A Paper

**LL:** What does it mean to be a leader? How might that differ across cultures?

*A brief lecture will occur about leadership and its
meaning.  Students will then engage in active learning
aligned with traditional and culturally responsive
learning goals.*

*A: Assignment Option 2 Answer Divergent Thinking
Questions*

**LL:** When was a time you had a leader that was not
effective?  How did that affect you personally, as well
as the organization?

**A:** Five-minute video discussion with or without a
PowerPoint.

## Administrative Case Study

*LaTonya is an administrator.  She explains
the different uses for each CRS to her team.
The course is designed for cultural
responsiveness (Tiera 1).  Individuals made
more connections with the content because
there were culturally recognizable or relevant
considerations within the content, scope, and
curriculum, as well as increased inclusion
during collaborative experiences (Tier 2).*
*Instead of sending the individuals to the
CTL or other organizational resources,
LaTonya suggests the team try something
different.  Because the group desired culturally
responsive feedback, LaTonya reminded her*

*staff that cultural responsiveness is optional
(Tier 3); the individual will say either, "yes, I
want culturally responsive feedback in addition
to the standard level of performance feedback,"
or "no, I am declining," or "I would like to go to
the standard level of feedback for my
evaluation."*

*LaTonya also noted some institutions
inherently run at Tier 3 because there is so
much familiarity and understanding of culturally
responsive design using this model. Cultural
responsiveness is embedded in the college
structure in many areas – examples being
Hispanic Serving Institutions (HSIs),
Historically Black Colleges and Universities
(HBCUs), and First Nation Serving Institutions
(FNSI). These institutions have cultural
responsiveness teaching specifics to help
move that concept into the academic space
and beyond the professional, social, or
collaborative space.*

## Putting It Together

The Tier system allows for identifying
evidence-based responses to find a home within one
of the Tiers. The Certified Culturally Responsive
Evaluation Specialist (CASEPS) standards support
the framework for CRS (2014). The Tiers are what,
when, and how for both instructors and designers:

- What strategy, response, or intervention is selected?
- Where was it applied (design, instruction, remediation, evaluation, feedback?
- How often was it applied?
- What strategy made individuals the most responsive in the learning environment?

The purpose of the Tier system is to increase cohesive, documentable, and effective processes. The CRS model classifies and identifies specific strategies of cultural responsiveness. This model contributes to the reduction of acculturative stress that impacts learning. While many other experiences contribute to a individuals levels of acculturative stress, these systems help focus on one's abilities to apply cultural responsiveness effectively in educational environments.

Models of cultural responsiveness exist. CRS is not just another model. The CRS model is a system that faculty and instructional designers can consistently and strategically apply for best practices in learning spaces.

# Chapter 6

## Tier 1, 2, and 3: Additional Considerations

### Tier 1: Whole Group Conceptual Considerations

Knowledge acquisition is essential for learning. A Eurocentric view of knowledge acquisition is common in educational practice (Booker et al., 2015). "For students to acquire new knowledge, they need to witness a more knowledgeable 'other person,'....In this case, the instructor teaching using the strategy being demonstrated" (Fisher & Frey, 2008, p.17) is one such example. There are many more examples in the general body of literature. Foundational practices highlight the 'sage on stage' framework highlighting a significant power imbalance and acknowledgment of cultural differences.

However, According to Arruzza and Chau (2021), "data relating to the skills domain demonstrated positive effects for learners after experiencing culturally responsive interventions. Individuals were satisfied with their experiences and demonstrated improvements in confidence and attitudes towards culturally competent practices" (p.1).

Secondly, knowledge acquisition is dependent on the delivery of the knowledge for acquisition. Two conceptualized modes for delivering knowledge are *pedagogy* and *andragogy*. It is important to provide distinctions between andragogy and pedagogy. Each word is often used interchangeably in education. Figure 19 highlights the basic differences between the terms (*pedagogy*, the teaching of children, and *andragogy,* the teaching of adults). The application of each term applies differently to the concept of whole group instruction and course design.

For instance, educational professionals often apply the term pedagogy when discussing best practices in education. The term pedagogy is also aligned with Eurocentrism and cultural norms (De La Torre, 2017). The repeated application of the term pedagogy creates an unsafe learning environment because it narrows applications of cultural responsiveness within teaching and course design. The environment is unsafe for two reasons: (1) Eurocentrism and (2) because it increases a power dynamic like that of adult vs. child. Childhood is where trauma often resides and where most emotional memory is aligned.

Educators internalize frameworks (Ibrahim & Abadi, 2018). Pedagogy is no exception. Educators who have internalized a pedagogy framework, embed maladaptive frameworks within their courses and then express concern about 'coddling students' or complain about reducing "student responsibilities." In essence, the framework of pedagogy is, in most instances, a developmentally inappropriate framework for learning. This maladaptive framework occurs because Eurocentrism is at the center of pedagogy and because developmentally the framework is in appropriate. Because of the inappropriateness of the framework, some adults display 'inappropriate' cultural responses in the learning environment because the mythology, framework, and dynamic support such responses. Instructor beliefs about 'inappropriate' responses perpetuate stereotyping, microaggression, racism, and blaming/shaming on the instructor's part and create a less than optimal learning environment. Additionally, an pedagogy framework creates an unhealthy and systematic point of power.

The framework for cultural responsiveness is no different. Culturally responsive course design and teaching frameworks are often framed using pedagogy. Andragogy is a more useful framework for applications of culturally responsive teaching and design practices.

*Figure 19 – The Differences Between Andragogy and Pedagogy*

| Domain | Andragogy | Pedagogy |
|--------|-----------|----------|
| **Content** | Places more focus on the student's desire for self-motivation by using their specific ways of learning. | Content and subject matter remain the focus of the education process. |
| **Learner** | Importance of social roles and how learners will learn within collaborative settings. Presenting | Learner is expected to complete take-oriented activities. |

| Domain | Andragogy | Pedagogy |
|---|---|---|
| | opportunities for learning within contextual and collaborative settings. | |
| **Role of Instructor** | Use problem solving and skills. | Students are highly dependent on directions of instructors and peers. |
| **Learning** | Apply a range of applications for learning and knowledge acquisition. | Learning is subject centered and toed directly to the content and learning outcomes. |

Because the framework pedagogy was originally constructed within homogenous learning environments, it is rooted in an ethnocentric context. Because of ethnocentrism within the framework, pedagogy practices equal power. Once an individual has identified and internalized pedagogy as a power and control model, it is extremely difficult to adopt additional practice because the power dynamic favors a culture of control (adult to child). The concepts associated with pedagogy are used to consistently promote the disregard of cultural responsiveness within the educational framework. Below are common comments associated with the internalization of pedagogy as a power dynamic.

- Content and subject matter remain the focus of the education process.

- o *"I teach math. There is no room in my curriculum for cultural responsiveness. I don't see the point."*

- o *Why do we have another training on cultural competency? I treat all my students the same way. I teach them how to write."*

- o *"I am not changing my curriculum because of the current political climate. This is all political nonsense."*

- Learner is expected to complete take-oriented activities.

  - o *"I am tired of reaching out to my students. They never turn in their work. If they would just turn in their work, I would, work with them. It is so frustrating that students do not want to engage in the course."*

  - o *"If all work is not completed by the end of the term, you will receive zeros in the gradebook."*

  - o *"No one reads the feedback. I continually re-direct my students back to the prior feedback until I see they have read the feedback and applied it."*

- Students are highly dependent on directions of instructors and peers.

  - o *"This is an asynchronous course. I spelled out everything in the directions. They never read the directions. If they just read the directions, they would know what to do…"*

- o *Post your question in the chat. I will respond within 48 hours.*

- o *"All important information (policy focus) is found in the syllabus."*

- Learning is subject centered and tied directly to the content and learning outcomes.

  - o *"By the end of this course students will be able to……*

  - o *"That is a great question, but it really isn't what we are talking about, here."*

  - o *In order to move on to part 2, you will need to successfully complete part 1."*

For individuals from systematically marginalized communities, pedagogical applications contribute to developing unsafe learning spaces. Such practices elicit cognitive patterns of self-protection within the learning environment. Individuals from systematically marginalized communities learn to protect themselves psychologically and/or physically early in life (Bagdanova, Rusyaeva, & Vyelgzhanina, 2016). Additionally, self-protection mechanisms are learned from mothers (Bagdanova et al, 2016). Women of color are significantly traumatized in many communities before the age of 18. Individuals from marginalized communities are more likely to psychologically protect themselves in a pedagogy-framed learning environment than engage in the learning process, especially if systematic marginalization and acculturative stress is present to a marked degree.

The use of pedogeological practices with adults, in most instances, brings feelings of trauma associated with racism and microaggression within previous learning experiences to the forefront, especially if the trauma occurred in childhood. The pedogeological model reinforced the need for self-protection. This is because emotional memories are often tied to cultural responsiveness or its absence in the learning environment. Moreover, victims of racism, marginalization, and microaggressions may experience cognitive 'numbness' (Ducet & Rovers, 2009) in the learning environment because the trauma associated with past pedological practices resulted in high levels of acculturative stress.

*Figure 20 - Tier 1 CRS© Applications*

| CRS© Applications | |
|---|---|
| **Tier 1: Who is involved?** LODEls, Instructional Designers, Practitioners, and Students | |
| **What's the Purpose?** | To add up to 20% of cultural responsiveness to a course. |
| **How will it happen?** | Development of culturally responsive goals, content selection, course design, community considerations |
| **Types of Culture** <br> ▪ *Academic* <br> ▪ *Community* <br> ▪ *Ethnic/* <br> ▪ *Intersectionality* <br> **A.C.C.C.E.** | **Academic culture:** Belongingness, inclusion, equity, self-identity (planning, announcements, content, policy) <br> **Community culture:** Learners as stakeholders, decision makers, and |

| CRS© Applications | |
|---|---|
| | care takers (Sense of Community, Climate, Community, and Course Ecosystem) |
| **Which students?** | All students have access minimal forms of cultural responsiveness and opportunities to build cultural competency. |
| **Ethnic culture and Intersectionality:** Student engagement, motivation, cognitive and social presence, learning, and memory. (All aspects of course planning, design, and instruction) | |

## Tier 2: Conceptual Considerations

As stated earlier, self-protection mechanisms are learned through social learning. Collaborative learning is social learning. Collaborative learning is a type of social learning that engages people with their peers (Higher Education Report, 2014). Contextual learning is a type of social learning that uses the environment to obtain information associated with cultural norms (Migliorini, Rania, & Cardinali, 2015). Both collaborative and contextual learning opportunities provide psychological and social support in the learning environment (Migliorini et al., 2015). Including cultural responsiveness to collaborative learning experiences influence the psychological, academic, and social factors associated with successful outcomes for students of color (Zvolensky, Jardin, Garey, Zuzuky, & Sharp, 2016).

Tier 2 cultural responses include evidence-based frameworks with cultural adaptations. Below is a cohesive and transparent methodology for measuring or documenting the impact of cultural responsiveness. Tier 2 focus is on the design of entry and a focus on inclusion as it relates to well-being and successful completion. The content below is an added entry into small groups, conflict resolution, group functioning, and development.

- **Collaborative culture:** Group forming and norming, participation, outcomes, interpersonal communication, and socialization. (Collaboration-Group Membership)

Although these practices are for all people, individuals drive how they will use the strategies. In many instances, people are randomly assigned to groups for collaborative learning. Regardless of how people are placed in groups, collaborative activities require cultural considerations of leadership development, conflict resolution, and group norming (how people position themselves in a group to feel included).

Administration, faculty, design teams frequently overlook the importance of group development from course design and instructional practices. Instead, faculty and course designers should place focus on the process of group development. In other words, how and why individuals select entry into a certain group, how they respond to the group upon entry, and responses within the group once the group has begun to engage in collaborative learning. Figure 21 highlights the Tier 2 process and who is involved.

*Figure 21 - Tier 2 CRS© Applications*

| CRS© Applications | |
|---|---|
| **Tier 2: Who is involved?** Instructional Designers, Practitioners, and Students | |
| **What's the Purpose?** | To add up to 50% of cultural responsiveness to a course. |
| **How will it happen?** | Assignment design, course norms, social norms, and group development. |
| **Types of Culture**<br>▪ *Academic*<br>▪ *Community*<br>▪ *Ethnic*<br>**A.C.C.E.** | **Collaborative culture:** Group forming and norming, participation, outcomes, interpersonal communication, and socialization. (Collaboration-Group Membership) |
| **Which students?** | Individuals who need more than tier 1 (general cultural responsiveness). |
| **Ethnic culture and Intersectionality:** Student engagement, motivation, cognitive and social presence, learning, and memory. (All aspects) | |

Individuals needing cultural responsiveness in Tier 2 will require specific cultural attributes to be present. It is important to provide activities that help individuals engage by culturally positioning themselves in a group. Those who may not need as much cultural responsiveness would do well with random assignments.

The common practice of random group assignment is often void of cultural considerations. Figure 21 highlights some of those considerations for culturally responsive collaboration.

*Figure 22 Tiers and Group Development*

| Tier 1 | | Tier 2 | Tier 3 |
|---|---|---|---|
| Assimilation | Integration | Separation | Marginalization |
| Random Group Development | | Culturally Responsive Group Development | |

Common practices associated with collaborative and contextual learning differ from those of culturally responsive practices. Common practices of collaborative learning, like whole group instruction, were developed in a Eurocentric framework (see figure 23).

*Figure 23 - Common Practice vs Culturally Practices*

| Domain | Common Practice | Culturally Responsive Practice |
|---|---|---|
| Content | Content is reflective of 'traditional" viewpoints. | Content is reflective of diverse author's and viewpoints. |
| Learner | Task-Oriented Learning | Collaborative and Contextual Learning |
| Role of Instructor | Facilitate learning: Students are highly dependent on directions of instructors and peers. | Facilitate students' ability to create culture within the group for a sense of inclusion. Interdependence is also valued. |
| Learning | Learning is task oriented. Leadership roles do not consider cultural differences. | Learning occurs through collaborative and contextual cultural collaboration. (See Tier 2 case study) |

## Tier 3: Conceptual Considerations

Tier 3 levels of cultural responsiveness are less common than Tier 1 and 2. Tier 3 includes cultural responses with cultural adaptations and recommendations for individual students based on the psychological evaluation process conducted by a licensed/certified mental health clinician. Following is a cohesive and transparent methodology for measuring or documenting the impact of cultural responsiveness.

Tier 3 levels of intervention are applied less often because of a lack of appropriately trained clinicians. The evaluation and clinical documentation of acculturative stress levels meeting the criteria 'marked degree' allow acculturative stress to be viewed as more like a disability within the learning environment rather than an afterthought or something individuals should learn to 'deal with.' Additionally, individuals may experience high levels of acculturative stress inside or outside of the academic environment or workplace. Cultural responsiveness to the academic environment would be different if the acculturative stresses were occurring in the workplace rather than the learning environment.

Tier 3 focuses on the design and an individual's learning style as well as, how culture can influence one's ability to learn and thrive within an environment.

- **Cognitive culture:** This includes decision

making, emotions, impressions, perception, attention, and cognition. (Instruction/Active Learning/Divergent Thinking).

Tier 3 is highly specialized and involves a screening or evaluation process.  This process would also involve one's understanding cultural responsiveness and understanding the levels to which it can support them in an educational or professional environment if needed and/or desired.

*Figure 24 - Tier 3 CRS© Applications*

| CRS© Applications | |
|---|---|
| Tier 3: Who is involved? Students, Clinicians, Instructors, LODEIs | |
| What's the Purpose? | Require 50% or more of cultural responsiveness to a course. |
| How will it happen? | Across all areas of education. |
| Types of Culture <br> • *Academic* <br> • *Community* <br> • *Ethnic* <br> A.C.C.C.E. | Cognitive culture- This includes, decision-making, perception, attention, thinking, knowing, and understanding. (Instruction/Active Learning/Divergent Thinking). |
| Which students? | The students need tier mild to moderate level of acculturative stress. |
| Ethnic culture and Intersectionality: Student engagement, motivation, cognitive and social presence, learning, and memory. (All Aspects) | |

Individuals experiencing acculturative stress are often sent to counseling or support professionals that are not reflective of themselves or their experiences.  Most frequently, individuals experiencing high levels of acculturative stress require cultural responsiveness to help decrease the acculturative stress. Instead, a Tier 3 model includes measured and specific supports for students with high levels of acculturative stress. Figures 25 and 26 highlight student services tiers of cultural responsiveness.

*Figure 25 - Student Services vs. Cultural Responsiveness*

| Tier 1 | | Tier 2 | Tier 3 |
|---|---|---|---|
| Assimilation | Integration | Separation | Marginalization |
| Tutoring Center | | Culturally Responsive Learning Interventions | |

Student services and cultural responsiveness are rarely discussed. Student service professionals like academic advisers are often left out of the conversations regarding cultural responsiveness. Similar to Tier 1, 2, and 3 teaching practices, Tier 1, 2, and 3 cultural responsiveness supports the cultural considerations associated with successful student service outcomes.

*Figure 26 - Tier 3 Culturally Responsive Practices*

| Domain | Common Practice | Culturally Responsive Practice |
|---|---|---|
| Content | General content with little cultural consideration | Content with same learning goals, different cultural viewpoint |
| Learner | Historical Learning Methods | Learning alternative was of learning through a cultural lens. |
| Role of Instructor | Facilitate learning: Grading and critiquing of | Facilitate learning: Grading and critiquing of the cultural values and measured to |

| Domain | Common Practice | Culturally Responsive Practice |
|---|---|---|
| | Eurocentric values. | support learning of content |
| Learning | Eurocentric methods of tutoring have unhealthy power dynamics. | Faculty and designers provide various culturally responsive methods to approach material via culture: problem solving, validation, etc. |
| *It is not recommended for any faculty member to conduct tier 3 practices without proper acculturative stress assessment. Doing so could cause negative outcomes and unattended consequences. Please check with your campus to see the resources available for this level of intervention. * | | |

Results of acculturative stress evaluations could be quantified and shared within the department of disabilities and institutions with the permission of the individual to support culturally responsive supports in the classroom (see Appendix A). Such evaluations should include:

- Name, Birth, Date
- Evaluation Date
- Evaluators Name and Qualifications
- Multicultural Ethnic Identify Measure
- Classroom Observations (Online and/or Face-to-Face; a minimum of two observations on two different dates)
- Psychometric Measures of Acculturative Stress, Marginalization and Socialization and other relevant psychometric measurements reflective of associated cultural values
- Culturally Responsive Interview

- o Social and Family History
- o Prior School Experiences
- o Current Challenges and Goals
- o Results
- o Culturally Responsive Accommodations

## Putting It Together

There is always more to consider when we think about cultural responsiveness. This chapter presented additional considerations for the applications of cultural responsiveness. The concepts presented in this chapter also help educators move beyond theoretical or topical concepts of cultural responsiveness.

Cultural responsiveness is an essential feature of teaching and learning. "A model of cultural responsiveness which avoids a deeper appreciation and advanced understanding of the complexity of race, cannot fully produce competent professionals equipped to provide effective services to racial and ethnic minority populations" (Campbell, 2015, p.25).

# Chapter 7

## Cultural Responsiveness, Equity, Access, and Accommodation

In 2021, Mark Nathan, Director of Assistive technology at Buffalo University, presented to the POD Network special interest group with the assertion that accommodations should not be viewed as compliance or strategic moves. But when done properly, accommodations should be viewed through the lens of equity and access within the learning environment, not compliance. Nathan also noted more than 40 million dollars should be invested in academic technology because it is a capital investment and a matter of equity and inclusion. Cultural responsiveness deserves the same respect and acknowledgment in higher education, and the following explains why.

According to Plotts & Cohen (2021), making decisions about academic technology requires an intentional and thoughtful decision-making process and should have considerations for DEI. Accommodations, in conjunction with the office of disabilities, provide support via academic technology and other accommodations like additional time or private testing rooms. Such accommodations support individual learning outcomes when a documented psychological phenomenon impedes their ability to learn when compared to their neurotypical peers. Accommodations support students living with cognitive, emotional, physical, or psychological barriers that impede learning. For some individuals, it could be a diagnosis of epilepsy or dyslexia. For others, accommodations may provide support to individuals mental health-related issue like anxiety or schizophrenia for other individuals. Additionally, accommodations are issued for more benign barriers such as testing anxiety.

To receive accommodations in higher education institutions or in the workplace, individuals are required to obtain a psychological evaluation from a psychologist or other licensed mental health professional. Documentation from counselors or doctors for issues like a chronic disease to receive accommodations (e.g., additional testing time or testing in solitary conditions).

Obtaining such documentation may be difficult for systematically-marginalized and racialized individuals. This may include rural white students with disabilities or communities of color struggling with acculturative stress. Access difficulties include geographical proximity, financial constraints, or stigma. Additionally, a private psychological evaluation can cost between $500 to $1,500 (depending on location, region, and type of evaluation requested by the institution). In many instances, students try to submit a legacy report to the office of accommodations in higher education institutions. A legacy report is documentation of accommodations applied in the K12 setting. Often, legacy reports are rejected. Currently, there is no standardization of procedures for requirements of psychological reports across higher education institutions.

Many psychologists are unfamiliar with remote-testing practices, which burdens the learner to engage in the testing process. Evaluations are completed in short-time units over multiple days. This fractured schedule means individuals may have to make multiple trips (in some cases, hours away) to complete the evaluation process. Transportation may not be available at consecutive or random appointment times. The lack of access to evaluation services is also true for students who attend virtual campuses.

> *Section 504 requires recipients to provide to students with disabilities appropriate educational services designed to meet the individual needs of such students to the same extent as the needs of students without disabilities are met. An appropriate education for a student with a disability under the Section 504 regulations could consist of education in regular classrooms, education in regular classes with supplementary services, and/or special education and related services" (Office of Civil Rights, 2021).*

The broadness and generality of the 504 allow a variety of situations to which institutions in both K12 and higher education have applied.  As a school psychologist who has practiced within educational institutions and privately as a counselor, I have seen creative uses of Section 504 student accommodations.  A short list includes:

- Student-athletes with broken fingers who cannot write with their dominant hand.
- The death of a pet.
- Stress over a household move.

## Clinical Evaluations and Documentation of Acculturative Stress

The clinical evaluation of acculturative stress for psychoeducational purposes is imperative if supporting the learning process for individuals originating from systematically-marginalized communities.  With institutions seeking effective solutions to increase academic achievement, the assessment of acculturative stress as it relates to academic success can no longer be ignored.  An assessment conducted by a clinical practitioner specializing in acculturative stress would be of great value to individuals and institutions.  High levels of acculturative stress documented by valid measures could fall under the 504 or more specific accommodations.

Historically, educators have tried everything to

make students and employees successful ... with the exception of the weight and meaning associated with culturally responsive accommodations and support. Acculturative stress is a psychological phenomenon that causes depression, anxiety, and isolation that negatively impacts learning. Clinically documented, depression and anxiety fall under accommodation criteria. Current accommodations are granted for documented disabilities through the Americans with Disabilities Act (1990).

Acculturative stress generates adverse psychological, social, and academic outcomes equal to negative consequences for lack of accommodation for traditional disabilities. If something, such as a move across the street or a broken finger, requires consideration, then surely something as well documented as the impact of acculturative stress originating from life-time encounters with racism, marginalization, and inequality rise beyond the level of a broken finger.

Cultural responsiveness is significant accommodation for those experiencing acculturative stress. Cultural responsiveness decreases invisible yet present barriers to effective cognition and socialization in higher education institutions. Culturally responsive accommodations are recommended for individuals experiencing high levels of acculturative stress. Accommodations may include Tier 1, 2, and/or 3 practices or more common practices such as extended testing time.

Providing documentation about acculturative

stress and culturally responsive accommodations contributes to the increased well-being of individuals. If education professionals desire to increase the relevance and longevity of cultural responsiveness via clinical documentation, a meaningful, equitable, and culturally responsive shift in education will occur. Clinical documentation of acculturative stress further contributes to the clinical significance of 'lived experiences' that include racism, prejudice, and microaggressions within a learning environment.

Acculturative stress should be categorized as a disability, when present to a marked degree, because it can interfere with cognition and cause negative psychological outcomes when present to a marked degree (Collier, 2011). Acculturative stress is measurable. Results of a clinical evaluation can identify specific barriers in the learning environment for individuals. Barriers associated with specific culturally responsive accommodations can be identified. This is the foundation for the clinical process of building cognitive equity in education.

Similarly, as with current practice, accommodations provided to instructors and course designers help developing more culturally responsive learning experiences for individuals. The CRS approach allows meaningful support to be introduced in the learning environment.

Cultural responsiveness should be viewed as accommodation within higher education because institutional systems historically have contributed to and caused acculturative stress by way of systemic marginalization. The educational system [itself] is significantly more culturally responsive to Eurocentric culture (Pittman, Cho-Kim, Hunter, & Obasi, 2017). Kiselica (1998) also offered that "Caucasian students might find it helpful to work with a White faculty member serving as a role model as it pertains to multicultural issues and the development of culturally competent practice." But, "for students of color, the identified challenges include colleagues not as interested in multicultural issues, faculty uncomfortable with multicultural issues, and potential differences between developmental progress of students of color and domination of their cultural counterparts" (Kennedy, Wheeler, and Bennett, 2014, p. 14). This is because "recruiting and retaining faculty of color has been and continues to be a challenge for many institutions" (Diggs et al., 2009, p.37). Yet, the literature provides significant documentation about how issues of marginalization, racism, and sexism can be manifested as unintended barriers to navigating the tenure process successfully (Diggs et al., 2009).

**Benefits of Culturally Responsive Evaluations**

Should they wish and legally consent, individuals should have the opportunity to clinically evaluate the negative effects of acculturative stress and its impact on their professional lives and learning experiences. In practice, clinicians who specialize in multicultural practice are best suited for clinical evaluations of acculturative stress. Institutions should adequately evaluate and accommodate acculturative stress trained professionals. Applying accommodations or culturally responsive supports contributes to the following:

- Increases in motivation (Bui & Fagan, 2013; Civil & Khan, 2001; Dimick, 2012; Ensign, 2003; Tate, 1995)
- Increases in interest in content (Choi, 2013; Dimick, 2012; Ensign, 2003; Feger, 2006; Gutstein, 2003; Martell, 2013; Robbins, 2001)
- Increases in ability to engage content area discourses (Civil & Khan, 2001; Gutstein, 2003; Martell, 2013)
- Increases in perception of themselves as capable individuals (Robbins, 2001; Souryasack & Lee, 2007)
- Increases in confidence when taking standardized tests (Hubert, 2013; Chang & Berk, 2009)
- "Cultural targeting includes any adaptation of a program that makes it more relevant to a specific population" (Unger, 2012, p. 392).

Individuals should have open access to the appropriate culturally responsive accommodations that provide equity and inclusion in higher education. Clinical documentation construction from the influence of acculturative stress uncovers and highlights the specific cultural responses required for individuals experiencing acculturative stress.

**Findings from the Literature**

The following points from the literature highlight the need for a more comprehensive evaluation of acculturative stress.

- Acculturative stress contributes to the development and maintenance of psychological maladjustment, including anxiety and depression (Williams & Berry, 1991), suicidality (Hovey, 1998, 2000a, 2000b), and emotional distress after controlling for other types of general stress  (Menton & Harter, p.239)
- When acculturation experiences cause problems for individuals, acculturative stress occurs (Berry, 2003).  Acculturative stress is a negative side effect of acculturation.  It can produce a reduction of individuals' physical, psychological, and social health (Berry, Kim, Minde, & Mok, 1987).
- "Acculturative stress has been defined as the psychosocial stressors associated with being part of two conflicting cultures and the perceived need to conform to the host culture to avoid discrimination (Mena et al. 1987).
- "Acculturative stress is important to school professionals and paraprofessionals to consider when attempting to engage in

teaching and learning" (Castro-Olivo and Merrell 2012; Albeg & Castro-Olivo, 2014).

- "The importance of considering acculturative stress in providing culturally responsive interventions is implicit in the literature, which, although sparse, notes that acculturative stress is a unique risk factor that puts ethnic minorities, such as Latinos, at higher risk for negative social-emotional, behavioral, and academic outcomes" (Blanco-Vega et al., 2008).

- "The degree to which acculturative stress is experienced may vary, depending on several social (e.g., pluralism of the society) and individual factors (e.g., modes of acculturation, personality). For example, Smith and Silva (2011) found the association between ethnic identity and personal well-being was stronger among adolescents and young adults than among adults over age 40" (Park, Song, & Lee, p. 139)

- "Although research has emphasized individuals' different coping styles concerning general stress, little attention has been how students cope with stressful situations: particularly, those related to acculturative stress" (Ra & Trusty, p. 320).

- "There is evidence that acculturation strategies are linked to discrimination, with those experiencing high discrimination more likely to prefer separation, whereas those experiencing less discrimination prefer integration or assimilation." (Sam & Berry, 2010, p. 417)

- "Sociocultural adaptation significantly mediated the effects of integration, marginalization, and social support on psychological adaptation" (Ng, Tsang, & Lian, p. 94).

- In addition to acculturation, acculturative stress is an important factor influencing the mental health of Latinas/os in the U.S. (Katsiaficas, Suárez-Orozco, Sirin, & Gupta, 2013; Torres, Driscoll, & Voell, 2012).

- Acculturative stress and psychological adjustment have also been observed in Latina/o youth and Latina/o college students (Crockett et al., 2007; Capio et al., 2015, p. 211).

- "Acculturative stress arises from multiple aspects of the acculturation process, such as learning new and sometimes confusing cultural rules and expectations, dealing with experiences of prejudice and discrimination, and the managing overarching conflicts" (Sirin and Rice, 2013, p. 2).

- "Acculturative stress also arises from negative stereotypes and attitudes that the host culture might harbor about immigrants in general" (Mahalingam, 2006; Rumbaut & Portes, 2001).

- "Due to the increase in anti-migrant sentiment in America over the past decade, migrants to the United States face considerable prejudice in their everyday activities that adds to their acculturative stress (Esses & Hamilton, 2021; Deaux, 2006). Thus, acculturative stress involves not only the degree to which one struggles with negotiating cultural differences but also the challenges of discrimination and prejudice due to one's cultural background or country of origin" (Sirin and Rice, 2013, p. 2)

## Acculturative Stress and Societal Impacts

Acculturative stress contributes to other negative outcomes outside of the academic environment. Acculturative stress contributes to homelessness (NHCH, 2019), incarceration (NeMoyer, Wang, Alvarez, Caniono, Duarte, Bird, & Alegría, 2020), increased rates of victimization (Kim, 2019), negative mental health outcomes (Kim, 2019), eating disorders (Mickelson, 2006), and marginalization through the lack of cultural responsiveness of mental health services to address acculturative stress (Mendlson, Turner, & Tandon, 2010).

Systemic culture creates barriers to equitable education. Higher education leaders need to address the issue of acculturative stress using a purposeful and genuine lens that fosters a sense of responsibility to the well-being of systematically-marginalized and racialized populations attending the institutions in the United States and abroad.

## Clinical Diagnosis and Important Considerations

According to Paginana (2019), a fundamental difference between classification systems is that clinical diagnosis is mute regarding the need to consider such variables in this context of diagnosing people with mental disorders, whereas the *DSM-5* does alert mental health practitioners to not make a diagnosis in this context without considering the cultural variables potentially affecting the assessment and diagnosis of such disorders.

Experiences with racism, microaggression, and marginalization create feelings of distress. Acculturative stress has clinical features of three of the four D's (deviance, distress, dysfunction, and danger) that call for intervention and treatment. Acculturative stress contributes to psychologically and, at times, physically and psychologically *dangerous* environments for individuals of color. Acculturative stress contributes to dysfunction including poor communication, frequent conflict, and frequent emotional *distress*. Acculturative stress also causes dysfunction that interferes with daily living patterns (Kaholokula, Antonio, Ing, Hermosura, Hall, Willis, 2017). Experiences of racism contribute to a significant loss of motivation and comfort after such experiences (Joseph, Peterson, Gordon, & Kamarck, 2021). High levels of acculturative stress and systemic marginalization can cause people to be a danger to themselves via depression and suicide (Fickman, 2020) and, at times, those around them.

Recommendations should be clear and concise for disability services approval. Recommendations should include samples of potential culturally responsive Tier 1, 2, and 3, interventions for the student's understanding as well as more common accommodations.

Educators often feel paralyzed because the need for cultural responsiveness is often too broad and overwhelming. Individuals might surmise they cannot 'fix' the problem because they are unsure what to say, where to turn, or what to do. Sometimes students, faculty, and staff are in the same position with feelings of being overwhelmed. At other times, there are no resources to address the underlying issues associated with acculturative stress. A center specializing in evaluating acculturative stress and the appropriate accommodations can provide solutions. A preliminary discussion is recommended.

**Putting it Together**

The importance of cultural responsiveness as a 'prescriptive' model to decrease acculturative stress cannot be understated. Equity is lacking in the area of accommodations for racialized and systematically marginalized individuals. Evaluating acculturative stress allows individuals to receive documentation that clinically validates their lived experiences. In addition, the evaluations acknowledge evident or perceived systemic barriers within lived experiences. Such evaluations provide documentation for experiences that often are ignored or minimized for various reasons.

·

# Chapter 8

## Best Practices and Adapted Best Practices

Good best practices are simple. Here is a list of easy-to-remember best practices. When applying cultural responsiveness

**Start and Start Small.** *Sometimes we start with a bang, and then things go by the wayside. To that end, start small. Think about what you have read.*

- *Discuss it with a peer or colleague.*
- *Try a culturally responsive discussion question (Tier 1).*
- *Reflect on your resistance to cultural responsiveness if need be. Has it changed or been modified by what you learned from reading this book?*

**Work collaboratively.**

- *Find culturally responsive practitioners with which to work.*
- *Reach out to experts online.*
- *Work with trained practitioners. Take the guessing out of cultural responsiveness.*

- *Meet with student service professionals. Find out about culturally responsive initiatives on campus.*
- *Include colleges from all departments and subject matter.*

## Take your time.

- *Cultural responsiveness is not intuitive. It takes time, information, practice, and intentionality to become a strong cultural practitioner.*
- *Don't get overwhelmed. If you do, take a break, and come back to the work. The work will wait for you.*
- *Practice creating tiered learning in a sandbox before implementation.*
- *Have a peer reflect on it with you. A second, third, or fourth set of eyes does not hurt either.*

## Everything is best in 3, but 5 will also do.

- *Focus on three culture responses at the Tier 1 level, per course. But if you need or want to do more, and it is your first time, five cultural responses are acceptable. No more than five. Keep it simple.*

## Learn more.

- *Read, research, reflect, and repeat.*
- *Become a certified Learning and Online Diversity, Equity, and Inclusion Officer (LODEI).*
- *Become a certified culturally responsive instructor.*

- *Become a CASEPS trainer.*

*Training opportunities can be found on the website* www.uscaseps.org.

# Chapter 9

# Conclusion

Cultural responsiveness is the duty of educators and course designers working in higher education. Whether you are a faculty member, instructional designer, or faculty developer, possessing a robust understanding of cultural responsiveness and its role in the learning environment is critical to improving higher education systems. Due to the relentless efforts of diverse researchers who have validated measures, explored the unexplored, and focused on historically unheard voices, a system has emerged that lends more acute applications of cultural responsiveness.

Institutions are responsible for understanding, evaluating, and responding to acculturative stress and the cultural responses (primarily marginalization) that negatively impact student learning and climate within the institution. This book, and the contributions of ethnically diverse researchers, provide a practical, evidence-based model for applying cultural responsiveness in a documentable manner. CRS provides individuals with a valid and reliable framework for implementing cultural responsiveness across educational settings.

The experiences associated with acculturative stress are measurable. Acculturative stress can occur inside and outside the academic, cognitive, collaborative, or community culture. Cultural responsiveness is a practical accommodation that should be used within the systems of higher education and beyond.

Offices that approve accommodations are often called Disabilities and Access Services. Cultural responsiveness is a 'prescriptive model' for depression, anxiety, and isolation caused by acculturative stress (Mena et al., 1987). All are attributes that negatively affect one's ability to learn.

Cultural responsiveness improves academic outcomes for systematically marginalized, racialized, and systemically marginalized students. Yet these students are often denied access to evidence-based supports that have repeatedly demonstrated a value when applied appropriately. Such as in the case of cultural responsiveness because the Eurocentric learning culture is the dominant culture.

Using a Tier CRS system of cultural intervention supports cultural responsiveness as a 'reasonable accommodation' based on the extensive research on its positive and measurable effects on the learning environment. It is equitable and reasonable to extend time on tests, provide assistive technology, or accommodate alternative assignment lengths.

Implementing the gradual, intentional, and directed use of cultural responsiveness is critical to learning outcomes for systemically marginalized and racialized students attending academic institutions and those who work inside the institutions experiencing clinically significant levels of acculturative stress.

The CRS© system gives practitioners insight into how to effectively apply cultural responsiveness in pursuing equity and equality. Individuals experiencing acculturative stress need a culturally appropriate response. A solution was needed to combat the effects of acculturative stress and systemic marginalization through a lack of cultural representation and understanding associated with educational experiences.

The CRS model provides a meaningful and documentable process for applying cultural responsiveness with purpose. Understanding, implementing, and evaluating cultural responsiveness takes time. The CRS model can also extend to other cultural groups of intersectionality (e.g., LGBTA+, etc.).

Dr. Scott Wright (2021), from the University of Arkansas, is one such example. He has researched the social needs and experiences of LGBTQA+ students in online spaces. This work highlights the differences between identity and how that identity is used to create social presence among LGBTQA+ students. This work is critical to understanding the role of cultural responsiveness for LGBTQA+ students' learning can be supported when traditional supports are not available.

Extensive examples of 'do it yourself' cultural

responsiveness have left a random pattern of patchwork best practices. The CRS© model provides a way for individuals, practitioners, and institutions to fully explore the benefits of cultural responsiveness from an objective and meaningful lens.

*Consider.* Wherever you are on the continuum of cultural responsiveness, I hope you consider how cultural responsiveness is applied prior to reading this book. If you are an administrator, please consider the points from the professional standards discussed in this book. Support your teams.

*Reflect.* Think about what you are already doing that may fit into the Tier system. Can you see the gradual building of your cultural responsiveness? Can you see you and your colleagues going to a professional development event and learning more about using this approach? The responsibility now lies with you. Be intentional.

For too long, aspects of culture have been left behind or absent from educational models. For too long, cultural responsiveness was ignored. For too long, the value of unique differences among ethnic groups has been overshadowed by systemic Eurocentric cultural norms fueled by historical frameworks of racism. Cultural responsiveness effectively increases engagement, motivation, socialization, coping, and academic achievement. You now have the model for adding cultural responsiveness to your educational practice. Use it and thank you for reading!

# APPENDICES

# Appendix A

## Sample Evaluation of Acculturative Stress and Marginalization Levels

| **Name:** Keshia Smith | ***School:*** | XYZ Institution |
|---|---|---|
| **Age:** 18 years, 5 months | ***Grade:*** | Freshman |
| | ***Examiner:*** | Courtney Plotts, Ph.D. |
| ***Contact Dates:*** | 01/08/19, 01/09/19, 01/11/19 | |

## Referral Reason:

Keshia was referred to the cultural support and evaluation center to obtain information that may be helpful to support her in her academic journey at XYZ institution. Keshia spoke with a professor. Her professor suggested she meet with someone at the Culturally Responsive Evaluation Center to explore and evaluate her acculturative stress levels.

**Goal:** The result of this evaluation may provide insights and recommendations to Keshia and her professors to best support Keshia in her learning endeavors at XYZ university.

## Evaluation Procedures:

**File Review:** This is a review of the student's

cumulative folder to identify academic history information and previous services. This data may include K12 and/or post-secondary levels.

**Observations:** These observations are conducted systematically so the student and their peers could be compared on the type and degree of behaviors that hinder or foster learning in the post-secondary setting. Socialization, sense of community, group development, and course ecosystem may also be included in the observation. Observations are usually conducted across several settings within a schedule of time.

**Social Developmental History:** An interview with a student's parents/guardians/siblings (optional) or the student to learn about the student's early and current health, academic, and social development.

**Reported Lived-Experiences With Racism, Marginalization, Bias, and Prejudice**: This is a social review of the context and instances in which perceived racism, marginalization, and/or prejudice has historically impacted the learning and socialization process.

**Multi-Ethnic Identify Measure (MEIM) (Phinney et al., 1999):** Multigroup Ethnic Identity Measure (MEIM) as a measure of the subjective sense of membership in any group. The MEIM measures the strength of psychological and social proximity to the ethnic group of an individual.  Appropriate ages 12-55 respectively.

**Acculturative Stress Scale (Adapted) (Bashir and Khalid, 2020):** A Multi-dimensional Likert scale of 24 comprehensive questions helps identify levels of acculturative stress among those attending a post-secondary institution.

**Aspects of Identity Questionnaire (AIQ-IV) (Cheek et al., 1987):** The AIQ-IV measures characteristics of identity that represent the domains of personal and social identity

**Lifetime Experiences of Marginalization Scale (LEMS) (Duffy et al., 2019):** This brief scale measures feelings of marginalization throughout a lifespan.

**Service Motivation Scale: (Duffy et al., 2019):** A measures aspects of communal beliefs and behaviors associated with communal culture and collaborative behaviors.

**Becks Depression Inventory: (Beck, 1961):** The Beck Depression Inventory (BDI) is a 21-item, self-report rating inventory that measures characteristic attitudes and symptoms of depression

**Becks Anxiety Inventory: (Duffy et al., 1994):** A measures aspects of communal beliefs and behaviors associated with communal culture and collaboration.

*File Review:*

Currently, Keshia's grades in college range from A's to C's. She reported that for most of her academic career, she has been able to maintain an A or B average. Keshia noted she would have to go home or call her old school to get 'exact' records but reported it would be difficult for time and transportation issues. Keshi reported she had given consent for me to speak with her mother and/or father, who probably have a better memory about her educational experiences.

*Social and Developmental History:*

Keshia is an 18-year-old student currently attending XYZ university. She reports she was very excited to start college as the first in her family to attend but has feelings of isolation, depression, and anxiety. She feels this is impacting her ability to learn in the educational environment effectively.
To her knowledge, she was born healthy at a normal weight. Keshia reported her mother ran an in-home daycare, and her father owns and manages a mechanic shop. Both parents are in the home and are still married. Keshia has two brothers and one sister. When she was growing up, she reported that her parents were "tough" on them, and school was very important. She also played multiple sports.

Keshia denied any experiences with emotional, physical, or sexual trauma.

Keshia noted when she attended high school, it was difficult for her when peers started dating. Keshia was the oldest in her family, and her parents saved for her to attend a private school across town. Keshia noted this was a stretch for her family because of the cost of gas. Keshia shared there were some "tense" times in those years. Additionally, socialization at a new school was complex. There were few students and fewer instructors that looked like Keshia. She emphasized this was very difficult when it came to romantic interests.

Keshia shared that going to college was an easy choice. Although she is the first person in her family to attend college, she "felt" she was ready academically and socially. Keshia reported her most significant concerns were not letting her family down and doing well in class. When asked why she decided to attend XYZ college, Keshia stated it was close enough to home if anyone needed her help. Financially, it was the best option.

*Observations*

Keshia was observed on 3 different dates: xx/xx/xx, xx/xx/xx, and xx/xx/xx.

**Observation 1:**

**Online Observation**: Keshia was asked to log into a

Zoom meeting link. Keshia was observed reading, writing, and studying.

- The student was fairly organized, took a significant amount of time to read, and displayed difficulty staying on task. Someone in the environment asked Keshia if she could help complete a task in another room. Afterward, she came back to complete the task. Keshia then went on Facebook and checked messages.

## Observation 2:

Observation: Keshia was observed in Comp 101.

- The student sits in the middle of the classroom. Keshia is focused on the teacher but is observed often staring (unclear student focus). Students were asked to participate in a group. Keshia was randomly placed in a group of five peers. A general observation suggests that Keshia is the only person of color in her group. It was also noted Keshia sat in the front right corner of the class.

## Observation 3:

Social Observation: Keshia was observed in the common area.

- Keshia was observed talking to multiple peers of color, and she seemed to be relaxed while she and her peers listened to music. They also had other friends enter and exit the group that appear to be of a different ethnic group(s). Handshakes and high-fives were exchanged. Keshia appeared to be comfortable and confident during this experience.

## Testing Observations:

Keshia came for testing on 1/26/22. During the testing, she was cooperative and friendly. She was very open to completing the scales and understanding how acculturative stress may play a role in her academic success. All questions were answered. At times, Keshia asked for clarity on questions she did not understand.

## Lived-Experiences:

Keshia reported in her experiences, being black results in experiences of prejudice, bias, marginalization, and racism. In the beginning, Keshia was vague about those experiences, except with her middle school and high-school dating experiences. Middle and high-school dating was difficult within the school setting. This was because she liked 2 boys during middle and high school, but she reported colorism from African American and white peers impacted her in negative ways. However, after general discussion and probing, three experiences emerged that help frame Keshia's previous experiences with such topics and how they impacted her sense of self.

**Experience 1:** In kindergarten, Keshia was playing with a student. The purpose of the lesson was to learn sharing by moving around as peers. Keshia was paired with a student named "Alissa." Keshia stated Alissa told her she "was not allowed to play with black people because they are bad." Keshia reports feeling "very sad" about this incident. She reported the first thing she was thinking was that her parents and siblings were "good people," and she did not understand why someone would say that. Keshia notes, she still remembers everything about that day.

**Experience 2:** Keshia shared that there was a lot of talk about this particular dress store in high school during prom season. Many of the students in her class went there. She recalls walking down the hallway and hearing a student comment: "Her mom likes shopping there because there are no "ghetto" people there, like the people who live in Townville," which is where Keisha's family lives. Keshia reported that many students thought poorly of her neighborhood, and comments like these were common.

**Experience 3:** Keshia reported that she had met more friends of color while attending XYZ college, which has helped. She noted that there had not been an "incident that she can recall at this time at XYZ college," but she reports feelings of not belonging and anxiety. She also has reported feeling "down" and "disconnected."

## Assessment Information

### Multi-Ethnic Identify Measure (MEIM) (Phinney et al., 1999):

**Multi-Ethnic Identity Measure results follow:**
Reported Ethnicity: African American
Father's Ethnicity: African American
Mother's Ethnicity: African American

| Ethnic Relativity | Standard Score | Percentile Rank | Descriptor |
|---|---|---|---|
| African American | 3.7 | 75-100th | High Level of Ethnic Identify and Relativity |

### Aspects of Identity Questionnaire (AIQ-IV): The AIQ-IV measures characteristics of identity that represent the domains of personal and social identity (Cheek & Briggs, 1981, 1982).

### Subtest results follow:

| | Raw Scores | Range | Descriptor |
|---|---|---|---|
| Personal Identity | 36 | 36-41 | Low |
| Relationship Identity | 38 | 35-40 | Low |
| Social Identify Identity | 21 | 21-24 | Low |

|  | Raw Scores | Range | Descriptor |
|---|---|---|---|
| Collective Identity | 32 | 29-34 | High |

## *Acculturative Stress Scale (Adapted) (Bashir & Khalid, 2020): Measures Acculturative Stress Levels*

| Domains | Standard Score | Percentile Rank | Descriptor |
|---|---|---|---|
| Academic | 103 | 58 | Highly Elevated |
| Local Living and Finance | 112 | 79 | Elevated |
| Culture and Religion | 100 | 50 | Average |
| Language Communication | 96 | 39 | High Average |
| Discrimination | 74 | 46 | High Average |
| **Acculturative Stress Scale Composite** | 105 | 63 | **High Average** |

## *Lifetime Experiences of Marginalization Scale (LEMS) (Duffy et al., 2019):* The LEMS measures marginalization, b based on specific group, have a specific identity, or life history. This often occurs due to one's gender, race/ethnicity, sexual orientation, disability status, religious beliefs, physical appearance, or being a part of other minority groups/identities.

| Ethnic Relativity | Raw Score | Percentile Rank | Descriptor Level |
|---|---|---|---|
| Marginalization | 7 | 100 | Extremely High |

***Service Motivation Scale(SMS) (Duffy et al., 2010):***
A measures aspects of communal beliefs and behaviors associated with communal culture and collaboration.

| Ethnic Relativity | Standard Score | Percentile Rank | Adaptive Level |
|---|---|---|---|
| African American | 4.6 | 80-100 | Extremely High |

***Becks Anxiety Inventory (BAI):*** The Beck Anxiety Inventory (BAI) consists of 21 items with a Likert scale ranging from 0 to 3 and raw scores ranging from 0 to 63. It was developed in 1988 and a revised manual was published in 1993 with some changes in scoring. The BAI scores are classified as minimal anxiety (0 to 7), mild anxiety (8 to 15), moderate anxiety (16 to 25), and severe anxiety (30 to 63). The BAI correlates highly with the BDI-II indicating that although the BAI may provide useful clinical information, it is not specific and can't be used diagnostically.

| Psychological Attribute | Raw Score | Percentile Rank | Descriptor Level |
|---|---|---|---|
| Anxiety | 36 | 66 | Potential Cause for Concern |

***Becks Depression Scale (BDI):*** The Beck Depression Inventory (BDI) is a 21-item, self-report rating inventory that measures characteristic attitudes and symptoms of depression (Beck, et al., 1961). The

BDI has been developed in different forms, including several computerized forms, a card form (May, Urquhart, Tarran, 1969, cited in Groth-Marnat, 1990), the 13-item short form and the more recent BDI-II by Beck, Steer & Brown, 1996.

| Psychological Attribute | Raw Score | Level | Descriptor Level |
|---|---|---|---|
| **Depression** | 13 | 2 | Mild Mood Disturbance |

## Conclusion and Recommendations

Keshia is an 18-year-old student who attends XYZ college. She was referred to the center for an evaluation to assist her in her academic endeavors. She reported increased feelings of anxiety, isolation, and lack of concentration.

Although Keshia historically has produced average or above-average academic scores, she currently is struggling to keep a grade-point average in that range. Keshia was referred by her instructor to the college's culturally responsive evaluation center. Keshia has reported she feels like "everything is catching up with her." Keshia reported she feels fairly good about attending the institution and has not been negatively impacted by racism, marginalization, discrimination, or bias per her interview. Her assessment scores however, demonstrate high levels of acculturative stress; marginalization is the response being used to manage that acculturative stress. Keshia's use of marginalization to manage acculturative stress negatively impacts her ability to perform academically.

Keshia may also be experiencing marginalization within the institutional system (acculturative stress academic score high average), although none was reported. This systemic marginalization could be further contributing to Keshia's feelings of isolation and depression. Although no prior history with depression and anxiety was reported, Keshia's marginalization scale scores were high, which increases the likelihood of depression and anxiety related to environmental or self-selected marginalization and is exacerbated by a lack of cultural responsiveness.

Keshia completed a Beck's Anxiety Inventory and Becks Depression Inventory. Both measures indicated depression and anxiety at clinically significant levels. Both may need to be proactively treated, or there could be short- and long-term impacts on her mental and physical health. Keshia may want to engage in counseling if her feelings associated with marginalization persist. Cultural responsiveness has been shown to decrease such feelings. It is recommended that cultural responsiveness within the social and academic environment may assist in reducing such feelings.

Keshia's scores on the AIQ-IV suggests she has a low sense of self-identity, with the exception of how her identity perceived in communal culture and identity that correlates with her Multiethnic Ethnic Identity Measure score. In other words, although

Keshia's ethnic identity is strong, that overall identity weakens in part due to high levels of systemic marginalization contributing to barriers for collaborative, social, and academic experiences.

Because of the discrepancies between Keshia's scores, as well as her reported-lived experiences and her scaled scores, it is suggested she would benefit from cultural responsiveness and interventions to support her learning. Keshia's overall Cultural responsiveness score is 3 (CRS 3). Meaning she will benefit from Tier 2, and 3 cultural responsiveness within the learning environment for the duration of at least one to two semesters.

Culturally responsive accommodations may benefit her throughout her time at XYZ college.

## Recommendations

## General Recommendations

1. It may be beneficial for Keshia to explore and possibly join multi-cultural clubs on campus. This extracurricular activity would provide additional support to discuss the specific realities of her experiences while also building social connections.
2. Keshia may also want to create specific schedule for checking in with friends and family members who reside on and off campus.

## Social Interactions

1.  It may be beneficial for Keshia to explore and possibly join multi-cultural clubs on campus. This membership would provide additional support to discuss the specific realities of her experiences while also building social connections.
2.  Keshia may want to explore her needs in a collaborative setting, making her feel more comfortable working in a group of homogenous and heterogeneous peers.
3.  Keshia may want to explore leadership concepts and how acculturative stress and marginalization have influenced her decision-making surrounding leadership vs. group member, career choices etc.
4.  Best practices highlighting the significance of the Keshia's awareness and skills as it relates to cultural responsiveness (Short and Williams, 2014).
5.  When requested, facilitate the socialization and learning process if/when needed (Short & Williams, 2014).

## Accommodations

1.  Keshia may need time to explore her needs in a group setting and what makes her feel most comfortable when working in a group of homogenous and heterogeneous peers.
2.  Keshia may also need to explore leadership

concepts and how acculturative stress and marginalization have influenced her decision-making surrounding leadership vs. group member.

3. Establish straightforward tasks in group activities. Allow Keshia to review those roles before group development occurs, possibly adjusting course assignments via the student's cultural lens.

4. Use culturally responsive goals to support Keshia's learning within the current academic framework.

## Academics

1. Keshia will benefit from a curriculum and assignment options that reflects her experiences and historical concepts that are reflective of her ethnic identity.

2. Keshia would also benefit from an online safe space for meaningful discussion that focuses on the community's current realities facing her community.

3. When struggling with an assignment, Keisha would benefit from culturally responsive academic feedback.

Courtney Plotts, Ph.D.
Director of The Cultural Responsiveness Evaluation Center, Certified and Licensed School Psychologist
Certified Culturally Responsive Evaluation Specialist (CASEPS)

# Appendix B:

## Accommodation for Cultural Responsiveness

**Student: Keshia Smith**
Student ID: XXXX
September 15, 2022
Professor Practitioner: English Department

Professor Practitioner:

I am writing concerning Keshia Smith (ID # XXXX), a student in your XYZ class.

Disability & Access Services has determined that Ms. Keshia Smith is a student with a disability and, based on the diagnosis and supporting documentation, the following accommodations are recommended:

## Accommodations

1. Use culturally responsive learning goals as alternative option assignments as needed.
2. Keshia may need time to explore her needs in a group setting and what makes her feel most comfortable when working in a group of homogenous and heterogeneous peers.
3. Keshia may also need to explore leadership concepts and how acculturative stress and

marginalization have influenced her decision-making surrounding leadership vs. her role as a group member.

# Appendix C

## The Practitioner's Planning Guide:
## Personal Reflection

Culturally Best Practices Questions for Reflection of Practice (Adapted from McGoldrick et al., 2008):

### Who
- Who is in the space? Who is defining the learning? Who is defining the barriers to the learning process? Do people within the learning environment share the same definition of learning? If not, what is different about it?

### What
- What is the actual problem vs perceived problem in the learning environment? Why are academic gains not occurring?

### Why Now
- What occurs that may be acting as an antecedent (the thing that prompts) acculturative stress to the learning happening in the classroom?

## History of The Problem

- Has this problem occurred for the instructor, course designer, or the student before this course?
- What is the expected response for both instructor and student?

## Cultural Heritage

- How do individuals' ethnic and racial backgrounds within the class contribute or impact their perceptions of the learning environment (expectations, inclusion)?

## Acculturation

- How quickly are individuals expecting/requiring people to adapt to academic learning environments? Might these expectations lead to marginalization or conflict?

## Socio-Cultural Norms

- What types of academic relationships are your collaborative assignments supporting? Distant, conflicted, interdependent?

## Community

- To what extent are individuals able to foster and maintain friendships and other peer relationships? How accessible are those friendships/relationships in online spaces vs. face-to-face communities?

- What cues elicit a sense of community?

## Learning Framework

- What cultural patterns and frameworks are embedded in your course climate?

## Potential Problems in the Learning Environment

- How might students get caught between the academic culture and the ethnic-cultural norms?

# References

Alankhunona, N., Dillo, O., Martin Del Campo, I., & Tallarico, W. (2015). *Defining marginalization. An assessment tool.* Elliot school of International Affairs.

Altugan, A. S. (2015). The effect of cultural identity on learning. Social and Behavioral Sciences, 190, 455-458.

American Psychological Association. (n.d.). Acculturative strategies. In APA dictionary of psychology. Retrieved January 18, 2018, from https://dictionary.apa.org/acculturation-strategies

American University (2019). Culturally responsive teaching strategies. Important benefits and tips. https://soeonline.american.edu/blog/culturally-responsive-teaching

Anderson, L. M., Scrimshaw, S. C., Fullilove, M. T., Fielding, J. E., & Normand, J. (2003). Culturally competent healthcare systems: A systematic review. American Journal of Preventive Medicine, 24(3), 68-79

Anonymous. (2016). Woodland joint unified school district. MTSS Guidebook. Student support and interventions.

Aronson, B., & Laughter, J. (2016). The theory and practice of culturally relevant education: A synthesis of research across content areas. *Review of Educational Research, 86*(1), 163–206.

Arruzza, E., & Chau, M. (2021). The effectiveness of cultural competence education in enhancing knowledge acquisition, performance, attitudes, and student satisfaction among undergraduate health science students: a scoping review. Journal of educational evaluation for health professions, 18, 3. https://doi.org/10.3352/jeehp.2021.18.3

Bai, J. (2016). Perceived support as a predictor of acculturative stress among international students in the United States. *Journal of International Students, 6,* 93-106. http://dx.doi.org/10.1037/pas0000198

Bandura, A. (1979). Social learning theory. Englewood Cliffs, NJ: Prentice Hall.

Bashir, A. & Khalid, R. (2020). Development and validation of the acculturative stress scale for Pakistani Muslim students.

*Cognate Journal, 7,* 1-5.

Beck A. T., Epstein N., Brown G., Steer R. A. (1988). An inventory for measuring clinical anxiety: psychometric properties. *Journal of Consulting and Clinical Psychology, 56*:893–897.

Beck, A. T., Steer, R. A., & Garbin, M. G. (1988). Psychometric properties of the Beck Depression Inventory: Twenty-five years of evaluation. *Clinical Psychology Review, 8*(1), 77-100.

Benabdallah, M. & Jolibert, A. (2013). L â acculturation: T'influence des sous-cultures d' origine et de la distance Culturelle. *Decsion Making, 7,* 179-205.

Berger, J. A., Heath, C., & Ho, B. (2005). Divergence in Cultural Practices: Tastes as Signals of Identity. Retrieved from https://repository.upenn.edu/marketing_papers/306

Berkeley S., Scanlon D., Bailey T. R., Sutton J. C., Sacco, D. M. (2020). A Snapshot of RTI Implementation a Decade Later: New Picture, Same Story. *Journal of Learning Disabilities, 53*(5) 332-342.

Blanco-Vega, C., Castro-Olivo, S. M., & Merrell, K. W. (2008). Social emotional needs of Latino immigrant adolescence: A socio-cultural model for development and implementation of culturally specific interventions. *Journal of Latino Education 7*(1), 43-61.

Bloom, B. S. (Ed.). (1956). Taxonomy of educational objectives: The classification of educational goals, by a committee of college and university examiners. New York: Longmans.

Bonebright, D. A. (2010). 40 years of storming. A historical review of Tuckman's model of small group development. *Human Resource Development International, 13,* 111-120.

Booker, K. C., Merriweather, L., & Campbell-Whatley, G. (2016). The effects of diversity training on faculty and students' classroom experiences. *International Journal for the Scholarship of Teaching and Learning, 10,* 1-7.

Booker, K. C., Merriweather, L., & Campbell-Whatley, G. (2016). The effects of diversity training on faculty and students' classroom experiences. *International Journal for the Scholarship of Teaching and Learning, 10*(1).

Brailas, A., Koskinas, K., Dafermos, M., & Alexias, G. (2015). Wikipedia in education: Acculturation and learning in virtual communities. *Learning, Culture and Social Interaction, 7*, 59-70.

Bui, Y. N. & Fagan, Y. M. (2013). The effects of an integrated reading comprehension strategy: A culturally responsive teaching approach for fifth-grade students' reading comprehension. Preventing School Failure, 57, 59–69. doi:10.1080/10459 88X.2012.664581

Bybee, R. (1997). Achieving scientific literacy. Portsmouth, NH: Heinemann.

Byrd, C. M. (2016). Does culturally relevant teaching work? Examination from student perspectives. Sage Open, 1-10.

Bogdanova, M. V., Rusyaeva, I. A., & Cylegzhanina, A. O. (2016). Gender and age aspects of child psychological definses in child-mother relationships. *Psychology in Russia* 9(3). Retrieved from http://psychologyinrussia.com/volumes/index.php?article=53 64

Burnham, K. (2020, 31st, July). Five culturally responsive teaching strategies. Retrieved from https://www.northeastern.edu/graduate/blog/culturally-responsive-teaching-strategies/

Campbell, E. L. (2015). Transitioning from a model of cultural competency toward an inclusive pedagogy of "racial competency" using critical race theory. *Journal of Social Welfare and Human Rights, 3*(1), 9-27.

Campbell, K., Kanuka, H., & Schwier, R. A. (2009, April). A preliminary study and research protocol for investigating sociocultural issues in instructional design. Paper presented at the annual conference of the American Educational Research Association, San Diego, CA.

Canton, C. The cultural taxation of faculty of color in the Academy. Service to the university and community. Retrieved from https://www.calfac.org/wp-content/uploads/2021/07/cultural_taxation_cfmagfall2013.pdf

Carss, W., Tamata, A., & Beryl, E. (2015). Catering for cultural and linguistic diversity: Using teacher created information texts. *Literacy Learning: The Middle Years, 23*(2), 29-40.

Carter, E. V. (2015). Delivering "virtual ethnicity" Drama: A pedagogical design for bridging digital and diversity barriers. *American Journal of Business Education, 8*, 327-348.

Chang, D. F., & Berk, A. (2009). Making cross-racial therapy work: A phenomenological study of clients' experiences of cross-racial therapy. Journal of Counseling Psychology, 56(4), 521–536. Retrieved from https://doi.org/10.1037/a0016905

Cheek, J. M. & Briggs, S. R. (1981, August). Self-consciousness, self-monitoring, and of Research in Personality, 16, 401-408.

Cheek, J. M., & Briggs, S. R. (1982). Self-consciousness and aspects of identity. *Journal of Research in Personality, 16,* 401-408.

Cheek, J. M., Smith, S.M., & Tropp, L. R. (2002, February). Relational identity orientation: A fourth scale for the AIQ. Paper presented at the meeting of the Society for Personality and Social Psychology, Savannah, GA.

Cheek, J. M., Tropp, L. R., Chen, L. C., & Underwood, M. K. (1994, August). Identity Orientations: Personal, social, and collective aspects of identity. Paper presented at the meeting of the American Psychological Association, Los Angeles, CA. Adapted from: Cheek, Underwood & Cutler (1985).

Chin, J. L. (2013). Diversity leadership: Influence of ethnicity, gender, and minority status. *Open Journal of Leadership, 2,* 1-10. doi.org/10.4236/ojl.2013.21001

Civil, M., & Khan, L. H. (2001). Mathematics instruction developed from a garden theme. *Teaching Children Mathematics, 7,* 400–405.

Choi, Y. (2013). Teaching social studies for newcomer English language learners: Toward culturally relevant pedagogy. *Multicultural Perspectives, 15,* 12–18. doi:10.1080/15210960.2013.754640

Conners family learning center. Boston College. (n. d.). Writing sample feedback. Retrieved from www.bc.edu/bc-web/academics/sites/connors-family-learning-center/writing-sample-feedback.html

Choudhury, I. (n. d.) Culture. Retrieved from http://people.tamu.edu/~i-choudhury/culture.html.

Cox-Davenport, R. A. (2014). A grounded theory of faculty use of humanization to create online course climate. *Journal of Holistic Nursing, 32*(1), 16–24.

Crockett, L. J., Iturbide, M. I., Torres Stone, R. A., McGinley, M., Raffaelli, M., & Carlo, G. (2007). Acculturative stress, social support, and coping: relations to psychological adjustment among Mexican American college students. Cultural diversity & ethnic minority psychology, 13(4), 347–355. Retrieved from https://doi.org/10.1037/1099-9809.13.4.347

Culhane, Stephen F. (2004). "An Intercultural Interaction Model: Acculturation Attitudes in Second Language Acquisition." *Centre for Language Studies 1*(1): 50-61.

Deci, E. L., & Ryan, R. M. (1985). *Intrinsic motivation and self-*

*determination in human behavior.* New York: Plenum.

De La Torre, M. A. (2017). The pedogeological failure of Eurocentric methodology. Retrieved from https://www.wabashcenter.wabash.edu/2017/05/the-pedagogical-failure-of-eurocentric-methodologies/

Diaz, C., Clarke, P. & Gatua, M. (2015). Cultural competence in rural nursing education. Are we there yet? *Nursing Education Perspectives 36,* 22-28.

Dimick, A. S. (2012). Students' empowerment in an environmental science classroom: Toward a framework for social justice science education. Science Education, 96, 990–1012. doi:10.1002/sce.21035

Dzubinski, L. M. (2014). Teaching presence: Co-creating a multi-national online learning community in an asynchronous classroom. *Journal of Asynchronous Learning Network, 18*(2),97-113.

Eagle, J. W., Dowd-Eagle, S. E., Snyder, A., & Gibbons-Holtzman, E. (2014). Implementing a multi-Tiered system of support. Collaborations between school psychologists and administrators to promote systems-level change.

Ecklund, K. (2013). First-generation social and ethnic minority students in Christian universities: Student recommendations for successful support of diverse students. *Christian Higher Education, 12,* 159-180.

Educational Alliance (n. d.). Teaching diverse learners. Culturally responsive teaching. Retrieved from www.brown.edu/academics/education-alliance/teaching-diverse-learners/strategies-0/culturally-responsive-teaching-0

Ensign, J. (2003). Including culturally relevant math in an urban school. Educational Studies, 34, 414–423.

Esses, V. M., & Hamilton, L. K. (2021). Xenophobia and anti-immigrant attitudes in the time of COVID-19. *Group Processes & Intergroup Relations, 24*(2), 253–259. Retrieved from doi.org/10.1177/1368430220983470

Fickman, L. (2020). *Racial discrimination linked to suicide.* University of Houston. Retrieved from https://uh.edu/news-events/stories/august-2020/08032020-rheeda-walker-racism-and-suicide-african-americans.php

Fisher, D., & Frey, N. (2008). *Better learning through structured teaching.* ACSD Publishing, Alexandria, VA.

Freeman, R. B. & Huang, W. (2015). Collaborating with people like me: Ethnic co- authorship within the US. *Journal of*

*Labor and Economics, 33,* 289-318.

Freeman, R., B., & Huang, W. (2014). Collaboration: Strength in diversity. *International Journal of Science, 515,* 305.

Fuchs, D., Fuchs, L. S., & Compton, D. L. (2012). Smart RTI: A Next-Generation Approach to Multilevel Prevention. *Exceptional Children, 78*(3), 263–279.

Garrison, D. R., Anderson, T., & Archer, W. (2010). The first decade of the community of inquiry framework: A retrospective. *The Internet and Higher Education, 13*(1–2), 5–9.

Garrison, D. R., Anderson, T., & Archer, W. (2010). The first decade of the community of inquiry framework: A retrospective. *Internet and Higher Education, 13,* 5-9.

Garrison, R. (2000). Theoretical challenges for distance education in the 21st century: A shift from structural to transactional issues. *The International Review of Research in Open and Distributed Learning, 1*(1).

Gay, G. (2010). Culturally responsive teaching: Theory, research, and practice (2nd ed.) (Multicultural education series). New York: Teachers College.

Guay, F., Vallerand, R., & Blanchard, C. (2000). On the assessment of situational intrinsic and extrinsic motivation: The situational motivation scale. *Motivation and Emotion, 24,* 175-213.

Gutstein, E. (2006). Reading and writing the world with mathematics: Toward a pedagogy for social justice. New York, NY: Routledge.

Hardin, E. E., Robitschek, C., Flores, L. Y., Navarro, R. L., & Ashton, M. W. (2014). The cultural lens approach to evaluating cultural validity of psychological theory. *American Psychologist, 69,* 656-668. doi:10.1037/a0036532

Heightner, K. L., & Jennings, M. (2016). Culturally responsive teaching knowledge and practices of online faculty. *Online Learning, 20*(4) 54-78.

Hill, A. L. (2012). Culturally responsive teaching: An investigation of effective practices for African American learners (Doctoral dissertation). Available from Proquest Dissertations and Theses Database. (UMI No. 3549438

Hovey, J. D. (1998). Acculturative stress, depression, and suicidal ideation among Mexican-American adolescents: Implications for the development of suicide prevention programs in schools. Psychological Reports, 83(1), 249–250. Retrieved from https://doi.org/10.2466/PR0.83.5.249-

250

Hovey, J. D. (2000). Acculturative stress, depression, and suicidal ideation in Mexican immigrants. Cultural Diversity and Ethnic Minority Psychology, 6(2), 134–151. Retrieved from https://doi.org/10.1037/1099-9809.6.2.134

Hovey, J. D. (2000). Acculturative stress, depression, and suicidal ideation among Central American immigrants. *Suicide and Life-Threatening Behavior, 30*(2), 125–139.

Hubert, T. L. (2013). Learners of mathematics: High school students' perspectives of culturally relevant mathematics pedagogy. *Journal of African American Studies, 18,* 324–336. doi:10.1007/s12111-013-9273-2

Ibrihim, M. A. (2018) Cultivating characters (moral value) through internalization of strategy of science in the classroom. *The Consortium of Asia-Pacific Education Universities.* Retrieved from https://iopscience.iop.org/article/10.1088/1757-899X/296/1/012047/pdf

Iris Center. Vanderbilt University. (n. d.). *What influence does culture have on a student's school success?* https://iris.peabody.vanderbilt.edu/module/clde/cresource/q1/p03/#content

Jenkins, S. R., Belanger, A., Connally, M. L., Boals, A., & Durõn, K. M. (2013). First-generation undergraduate students' social support, depression, and life satisfaction. *Journal of College Counseling, 16,* 129-142.

Johnson-Ahorlu, R. N. & Cuellar, M. (2016). Examining the complexity of the campus racial climate at a Hispanic serving community college. *Community College Review, 44,* 135-152.

Joseph, N. T., Peterson, L. M., Gordon, H., & Kamarck, T. W. (2021). The double burden of racial discrimination in daily-life moments: Increases in negative emotions and depletion of psychosocial resources among emerging adult African Americans. *Cultural diversity & ethnic minority psychology, 27*(2), 234–244. https://doi.org/10.1037/cdp0000337

Kaholokula, J.K., Antonio, M.C., Ing, C.K.T., Hermosura, A., Hall, K. E., Knight, R., Willis, T. A. (2017). The effects of perceived racism on psychological distress mediated by venting and disengagement coping in Native Hawaiians. *BMC Psychol 5,* 2 (2017). Retrieved from https://doi.org/10.1186/s40359-017-0171-6

Kennedy, J. A., Wheeler, W. N., & Bennett, S. (2014). An exploratory study of classroom diversity and cultural

competency. *Journal of Counselor Preparation &
Supervision, 6,* 7-20.

Kiselica, M. S. (1998). Preparing Anglos for the Challenges
and Joys of Multiculturalism. *The Counseling
Psychologist, 26*(1), 5–21. Retrieved from
https://doi.org/10.1177/0011000098261001

Kolb, D. A. (1976). *The Learning Style Inventory: Technical
Manual.* Boston, M. A.

Larson, K. E., Pas, E. T., Bradshaw, C. P., Rosenberg, M. S., &
Day-Vines, N. L. (2018). Examining how proactive
management and culturally responsive teaching relate to
student behavior: Implications for measurement and
practice. *School Psychology Review, 47*(2), 153-166 Lee, J.
K.L., & Green, K. (2012). Acculturation process of Hmong in
Eastern Wisconsin. *Hmong Studies Journal, 11,* 21-42.

Luyt, I. (2013). Bridging spaces: Cross-cultural perspectives on
promoting positive online learning experiences. *Journal of
Educational Technology Systems, 42,* 3-20.

Mackay, H. & Strickland, M. J. (2018). Exploring culturally
responsive teaching and student-created videos in an at-risk
middle school classroom. *Middle Grades Review, 4*(1), 1-15.
Maldonado-Torres, S. (2014). The relationship between
Latino students' learning styles and their academic
performance. *Community College Journal of Research and
Practice, 38*(4), 357–369.

Mareno, N., & Hart, P. (2014) Cultural competency among
nurses with undergraduate and graduate degrees:
Implications for nursing education. *Nursing Education
Perspectives, 35,* 83-88.

Martell, C. C. (2013). Race and histories: Examining culturally
relevant teaching in the U.S. history classroom. *Theory &
Research in Social Education, 41,* 65–88. doi:
10.1080/00933104.2013.755745

McGoldrick, M., Giordanio, J., & Garcia-Preto, N. (2005). Ethnic
and family therapy. Guilford Press. McMillan, D.W. & Chavis,
D. M. (1986). Sense of community: Definition and theory.
Journal of Community Psychology, 14, 6-23.

McIntosh, K., Craft, C. & MacKay, L. (2013). Perceived Cultural
Responsiveness and Effectiveness of a Speech and
Language Program for Indigenous Preschool Students.
Multicultural Learning and Teaching, 8(1), 47-64.

Menon, C. & Harter, S. (2012). Examining the impact of
acculturative stress on body image disturbance among

Hispanic college students. *Cultural Diversity and Ethnic Minority Psychology 18*(3) 239-246.

Mental Illness Policy Organization (2015). Extensive summary of the effects of untreated mental illness. https://mentalillnesspolicy.org/consequences/homeless-mentally-ill.html

Michigan Association of School Psychologists. (2000). *The role of school psychologists in the RtI process.*

Migliorini, L., Rania, N., & Cardinali, P. (2015). Intercultural learning context and acculturation strategies. Procedia - *Social and Behavioral Sciences, 171*, 374-381.

Morong, G., & DesBiens, D. (2016). Culturally responsive online design. Learning at intercultural intersections. *Intercultural Education 27* (5) 474-492.

Mykota, D. B. (2015). A replication study on the multi-dimensionality of online social presence. *Turkish Online Journal of Educational Technology, 14*(1), 11-18.

National Association of School Psychologists (2021). ESSA and Multi-Tiered systems of support for school psychologists. Retrieved from https://www.nasponline.org/research-and-policy/policy-priorities/relevant-law/the-every-student-succeeds-act/essa-implementation-resources/essa-and-mtss-for-school-psychologists

Ng, T. K., Tsang, K. K., & Lian, Y. (2013). Acculturation strategies, social support, and cross- cultural adaptation: A mediation analysis. *Asia Pacific Education Review, 14*, 593-601.

Ojeda, L., Castillo, L. G., Meza, R. R., & Piña-Watson, B. (2014). Mexican Americans in higher education: Cultural adaptation and marginalization as predictors of college persistence intentions and life satisfaction. *Journal of Hispanic Higher Education, 13,* 3-14. doi.org/10.1177/1538192713498899

Peterson, R. S., & Behfar, K. J. (2003). The dynamic relationship between performance feedback, trust, and conflict in groups: A longitudinal study. *Organizational Behavior and Human Decision Processes, 92,* 102–112.

Petty, T. (2014). Motivating first generation students to academic success and college completion. *College Student Journal, 48*(2), 257-264.

Phinney, J. (1992). The Multiple ethnic identity measure. A new scale for the use of adolescence and youth adults from diverse groups. *Journal of Adolescent Research, 7*(2) 156-176.

Phinney, J. S., & Haas, K. (2003). The Process of Coping Among Ethnic Minority First-Generation College Freshmen: A Narrative Approach. The Journal of Social Psychology, 143(6), 707–726. Retrieved from https://doi.org/10.1080/00224540309600426

Piaget, J. (1971). The theory of stages in cognitive development. In D. R. Green, M. P. Ford, & G. B. Flamer, *Measurement and Piaget*. McGraw-Hill.

Piazza, S. V., Rao, S., & Protacio, M. S. (2015). Converging recommendations for culturally responsive literacy practices: Students with learning disabilities, English language learners, and socioculturally diverse learners. *International Journal of Multicultural Education, 17*(3), 1-20. Plotts, C. (2020). *The Space Between: Identifying Cultural Canyons in Online Spaces and the use of Black Culture to Bridge the Divide* DCB Publishing.

Pittman DM, Cho Kim S, Hunter CD, Obasi EM. The role of minority stress in second-generation Black emerging adult college students' high-risk drinking behaviors. *Cultur Divers Ethnic Minor Psychol*. 2017;23(3):445-455. doi:10.1037/cdp0000135

Plotts, C. (2020). *The Space Between: Identifying Cultural Canyons in Online Spaces and the use of Black Culture to Bridge the Divide*. DCB Publishing.

Plotts, C. (2021). *Cultural presence: Applications for teaching and learning models in online spaces: Best practices* (1st ed.). CASEPS National Certification Curriculum.

Prause, D., & Mujtaba, B. (2015). Conflict management for diverse workplaces. *Journal of Business Studies Quarterly, 6*(3), 13-22. Retrieved from http://jbsq.org

Roberts, E. R., Phinney, J. S., Masse, L. C., Chen, Y. R., & Romero, A. (1999). The structure of ethnic identity of young adolescents from diverse ethnocultural backgrounds. *Journal of Early Adolescence, 19,* 301-322.

Rudmin, F. W. (2003). Critical history of the acculturation psychology of assimilation, separation, integration, and marginalization. *Review of General Psychology, 7*(1), 3-37.

Scholaske, L., Rodriguez, N., Sari, N. E., Spallek, J., Ziegler, M., & Entringer, S. (2020). The German Version of the Multidimensional Acculturative Stress Inventory (MASI) for Turkish-Origin Immigrants -Measurement Invariance of Filter Questions and Validation. European journal of psychological assessment: official organ of the European Association of

Psychological Assessment, 36(5), 889–900.
https://doi.org/10.1027/1015-5759/a000567Sirin, S., & Ryce,
P., Gupta, T., & Rogers-Sirin, L. (2013). The role of
acculturative stress on mental health symptoms for
immigrant adolescents: A longitudinal investigation.
*Developmental Psychology, 49, 736-748.*

Sirin, S. R., Gupta, T., Ryce, P., Katsiaficas, D., Suárez-Orozco,
C., & Rogers-Sirin, L. (2013). Understanding the role of
social support in trajectories of mental health symptoms for
immigrant adolescents. Journal of Applied Developmental
Psychology, 34(5), 199–207.
https://doi.org/10.1016/j.appdev.2013.04.004

Snowball, J. D. (2014). Using interactive content and online
activities to accommodate diversity in a large first year class.
*Higher Education, 67,* 823-838.

Soper, T., & Ukot, E. (2016). Social presence and cultural
competence in the online learning environment (OLE): A
review of literature. *American Journal of Health Sciences, 7,*
9- 13.

Souryasack, R. & Lee, J. S. (2007). Drawing on students'
experiences, culture and languages to develop English
language writing: Perspectives from three Loa heritage
middle school students. *Heritage Language Journal 5*(1) 79-
97.

Tate, W. F. (1995). Returning to the root: A culturally relevant
approach to mathematics pedagogy. Theory into Practice,
34, 166–173. doi:10.1080/00405849509543676

Torres, L., Driscoll, M. W., & Voell, M. (2012). Discrimination,
acculturation, acculturative stress, and Latino psychological
distress: a moderated mediational model. *Cultural diversity &
ethnic minority psychology, 18*(1), 17-25.

Thompson, C. P., Anderson, L. P., & Bakeman, R. A. (2000).
Effects of racial socialization and racial identity on
acculturative stress in African American college students.
*Cultural Diversity and Ethnic Minority Psychology, 6*(2),
196-210.

Tuckman, B. W., & Jensen, M. A. C. (1977). Stages of small-
group development revisited. *Group & Organization
Management, 2,* 419-427.

Urzúa, A., Henríquez, D., Caqueo-Urízar, A., & V., Smith-Castro
(2021). Validation of the brief scale for the evaluation of
acculturation stress in migrant population (EBEA).
*Psychology and Critical Reflection, 34*(3)

https://doi.org/10.1186/s41155-020-00168-3

VandenBos, G. R., & American Psychological Association. (2020). *APA dictionary of psychology.* Washington, DC: American Psychological Association.

Vigil, K., & Abedon, E. (2020). Designing equitable and culturally responsive learning spaces. *Aurora Institute.*

Warner, A. G. (2016). Developing a community of inquiry in face-to-face class. How an online learning framework can enrich traditional classroom settings. *Journal of Management Education 40,* 43 432-452.

Washoe County School District (n.d.). *Student learning objectives and instructional design strategies.*

Watson-Singleton, N. N., Pennefather, J. & Trusty, T. (2018). Can a culturally-responsive Mobile health (mHealth) application reduce African Americans' stress?: A pilot feasibility study. *Current Psychology.* Retrieved from: https://doi.org/10.1007/s12144-021-01534-9

Whiteside, A. (2015). Introducing the social presence model to explore online and blended learning experiences introducing the social presence model to explore online and blended learning experiences. Journal of Asynchronous Learning Network, 19(2), 53-73.

Wood, D. J., Bruner, J. S., & Ross, G. (1976). The role of tutoring in problem solving. *Journal of Child Psychiatry and Psychology, 17*(2), 89-100.

Woodley, X., Hernandez, C., Parra, J., Negesh, B. (2017). Celebrating difference. Best practices in culturally responsive teaching online. Tech Trends (61) 470-478.

Celebrating Difference: Best Practices in Culturally Responsive Teaching Online. TechTrends 61, 470–478 (2017). https://doi.org/10.1007/s11528-017-0207-z

Yin P, & Fan X. (2000). Assessing the Reliability of Beck Depression Inventory Scores: Reliability Generalization across Studies. *Educational and Psychological Measurement, 60,* 201-223.

Yin, R. K. (2010). *Qualitative Research from Start to Finish.* Thousand Oaks, CA: Sage.

# INDEX

virtual spaces, 25, 28
visual affirmation, 39

whole group instruction,
57, 60

# ABOUT THE AUTHOR

Dr. Courtney Plotts is a dynamic keynote speaker and presenter. Dr. Plotts has a Ph.D. in Psychology and, at the time of this writing, is the National Chair for the Council of At-Risk Student Education and Professional Standards. She was recognized by the California Legislation in 2017 for a change in education. Dr. Plotts consulted in the book, *Small Teaching Online* (Flower Darby and James Lang, 2019).

Dr. Plotts provides professional development sessions on best practices in cultural responsiveness teaching and mental health practices well practices in face-to-face and online environments. In 2020, she worked on the *Space Between* series of books focused on caring and connected behaviors in online spaces for black students and Latin students learning in virtual classrooms and spaces. These books were published between 2020 and 2022 and are available on Amazon. Dr. Plotts is also a practicing virtual school psychologist providing counseling and assessment service to students living in rural parts of the United States.

# ABOUT THE BOOK

It's another great read by Dr. Plotts. This book challenges educators to think about how they apply cultural responsiveness within the learning environment.

This book is a 'must-have' in for educators and instructional designers. Dr. Plotts addresses practical and intentional considerations for cultural responsiveness with learning psychology in mind as well as effectiveness and ease of use.

The idea of cultural adaptation to learning is critical to instructional effectiveness in online higher education environments. This book is an important read for administrators, staff and faculty alike.

This book provides clear foundations and examples of a specific viewpoint, background knowledge, and skills, as well as a framework for faculty, instructional designers, and curriculum developers to effectively enhance the practice of cultural responsiveness in educational settings.

Made in the USA
Middletown, DE
23 October 2022

13339156R00113